UNFORGETTABLE, UNFORGOTTEN

ANNA BUCHAN
(O. DOUGLAS).

UNFORGETTABLE, UNFORGOTTEN

By

ANNA BUCHAN

(O. DOUGLAS)

London HODDER & STOUGHTON Limited

FIRST PRINTED . . JUNE 1945
REPRINTED . . OCTOBER 1945
REPRINTED . . DECEMBER 1945

Made and Printed in Great Britain for HODDER AND STOUGHTON LTD., London
by WYMAN & SONS LIMITED, London, Reading and Fakenham

TO MY GENTLE READERS

You who read so faithfully my books may, perhaps, be interested in this family chronicle.

It was written in an effort to lighten dark days by remembering happier ones.

My brother John used to say that when he wrote stories he invented, but that I in my books was always remembering.

Here in this chronicle is the fount of all my memories.

ANNA BUCHAN.

(O. Douglas.)

ILLUSTRATIONS

7

CHAPTER I

· FIFE

> " . . . Do not think you can at all
>   By knocking on the window call
>   That child to hear you . . .
>   For long ago, the truth to say,
>   He has grown up and gone away,
>   And it is but a child of air
>   That lingers in the garden there."
>
> R. L. S.

IT is a help in dark days to remember bright beginnings.
Though, later, the clouds roll up, the sun is obscured
and all colour drained from the landscape, no one can
take from us the memory of a perfect morning. Oddly
enough, what I remember most clearly looking back
across the years is the night-nursery in the old Manse
in Fife : that seems to have been the spiritual home of
my childhood.

The day-nursery, with a snowball tree at the window,
and a cupboard full of toys (mostly broken), is only
associated with material things like porridge and bread-and-
butter, whereas the night-nursery had a magic casement.
One of the two windows looked across the garden and the
field beyond and a jumble of roofs, to the grey water of
the Firth of Forth and the Inchkeith Lighthouse. As the
darkening fell, we children clustered round to watch the
light come and go, convinced in our own minds that it
was caused by a giant waving a lantern. My bed was
alongside the fireplace, and from it I could see the twink-
ling light, and went to sleep every night thinking warmly
of the patient giant.

Willie and Walter and I shared the night-nursery. John,
the eldest, had a small room to himself, a sort of prophet's

9

chamber, containing only a bed, a chair, and a table. I did not envy him his lonely splendour. Being easily scared, I was only too thankful for the companionship of my two brothers ; · besides, if we woke early we had fine games, making an Indian tent in the boys' bed with our blankets and sheets. Once, having tied a sheet to the gas-bracket, and being too intent on our game to notice that the bracket had given away, and that gas was escaping, we were much surprised to see the panic-stricken face of Ellie Robbie (the nurse) as she rushed in and threw open the window, upbraiding us bitterly the while.

Opening out of the nursery was a small room with a fitted-in bath, and a window that gave a glimpse of the high road. It also contained the tallest soiled-linen basket that I have ever met. Willie once said, " If anyone comes to marry me, I'll hide in the dirty-clothes basket."

There is probably nothing a child values so much as a feeling of safety, and the night-nursery was the safest, friendliest room in the whole house. To reach it, when we went to bed, meant braving a dimly lit staircase and a long landing peopled, we were certain, not only by fabulous monsters of every description, but by all the most frightening book-people. The last few yards were always a frenzied rush, with a moment of terror in case the door would not open, and then—Ellie Robbie, moving quietly about in the firelight, our beds neatly made down, with the nightgowns laid out. In winter we wore nightgowns of red flannel, and when we heard of the Virtuous Woman in *Proverbs* who clothed her household in scarlet, we felt we could picture them exactly, down to the white herringboning on the belts and cuffs.

Ellie Robbie was such a kind and comfortable nurse (her real name was Ellen Robinson, and her father was believed by us to be the original of the saying, ' Before you can say Jack Robinson '), that bed-time was no bug-bear to us. In fact, the last half-hour of the day was something to look forward to, for Mother was nearly always with us, sitting on the low ' nursing ' chair, with the youngest on her lap, telling of what she did when she was little. Father often looked in too, and played us a tune, for, like R. L. S., he was a great performer on the penny-whistle! Sometimes he sang to us old Scots songs of which he had an inexhaustible store, or Negro songs about ' Way down South in the land of cotton,' or ' A coloured girl whose name was Nancy Till.' But what we liked best were the odd old rhymes that he had been taught as a child :

> " Cockybendy's lying sick,
> Guess ye what'll mend him ?
> Twenty kisses in a clout.
> Lassie, will ye send them ? "

and the long list of animals owned by one, Katie Bairdie, beginning :

> " Katie Bairdie had a coo
> A' black about the mou' ;
> Wasna that a denty coo ?
> Dance, Katie Bairdie ! "

There was one about a strange person called Aitken Drum. ' His breeks they were made of the haggis bags,' we were told, and ' his buttons they were made of bawbee baps,' and, strangest of all, ' he rade upon a razor.'

Being a passionate lover of his own countryside, Father never tired repeating to us the Border ballads ; how ' Jamie Telfer of the fair Dodhead ' carried the fray to Branksome Ha', and how Johnny Armstrong went out in all good faith to meet his King, only to find that death was to be his portion. He told us, too, of William Wallace, of Flodden Field, and Mary Queen of Scots, until we burned with fury against ' the English.'

Imagine, then, our horror and amazement when we were told that an English cousin was coming to us for a night on her way North. An *English* cousin! We had not known that such a thing existed, and we felt it shameful that we should harbour even for a night one of a race that had treated our country so basely. In herself she seemed harmless, a pretty creature, just grown up, whom, had things been different, we would have welcomed gladly, and to whom we would have been delighted to show our small treasures. But, as we stood and glowered, we were laying at this innocent's door all the ill-done deeds of her country —the head of William Wallace on a spike, the ring of dead nobles round their King at Flodden, not to speak of the cruel, lonely death of the loveliest Queen in history.

Doubtless she had been warned about Scots manners, and expected little; anyway, she only smiled at us—she had a beguiling smile—and went on making conversation with our parents, and we retreated to a lair of our own.

English Marjorie, we heard later, had not been favourably impressed with our house. She thought it ghostly, and dreaded sleeping alone.

There were two guest-rooms in the Manse, and Marjorie was in what we called ' besbedroom.' It was a large room furnished in some sort of golden wood much admired by Father. The dressing-table had a row of tiny drawers on either side of the looking-glass, and at Christmas time these were filled with small gifts for our stockings. It was quite an adventure before the great day came, to tiptoe in and keek at Santa Claus' store, and sniff that ' unforgettable, unforgotten' smell made up of lavender, beeswax-and-turpentine and chocolate frogs in silver paper.

There was also a large cupboard in ' besbedroom ' which we were afraid to enter, John having told us a dreadful story about it. To cheer homesick Marjorie on her way to bed, Mother had taken her with her to see that all was well in the night-nursery. There she had been so envious of me curled in my bed by the side of the fire and companioned by brothers, that she begged to be allowed to take me to sleep with her, and, Mother consenting, I had been carried, still sound asleep, to the large double bed.

The light was filtering in through the curtains when I woke, and at first I could not imagine where I was. The window was in the wrong place, the boys' bed was not there. I peered over the sheet. There was the towering wardrobe, the dressing-table with the rows of little drawers —I was sharing the bed of the English cousin.

An agonising loneliness came over me such as I have never again experienced. Samson bound in Gaza with the Philistines around him could not have felt more cut off from his own people than I did. It was not to be borne, so, very cautiously, I slipped from under the covers on to the floor. Skirting the writing-table, I passed safely the haunted cupboard and reached the door. The handle was difficult, and I glanced fearfully at the sleeper as I turned and twisted it; but at last it opened and I was free.

I did not dare go back to my own bed. The night-nursery was not safe from the marauding English; I would go to John. The door of the prophet's chamber stood invitingly open, and like a frightened rabbit I burrowed into his bed. Here was safety. In a minute I was asleep.

In the morning there were explanations. Mother apologised to our guest, explaining that I had wakened and missed the boys, and Marjorie bore no ill-will, and went off in high spirits, kissing us all in what we thought of as her ' English way.'

But Mother had been well aware of our coldness and antagonism the night before, and demanded to know what was the meaning of it.

We told her, and she looked at Father. "This is your fault, John," she said.

Father drew his hand over his mouth and acknowledged his guilt. "Yes," he said, "I'm the culprit. I've told them too many stories, taught them too many ballads."

Later, when he was taking us for a walk in the Den, he explained that all he had told us had happened long ago. "Why, you silly little people, don't you know that England and Scotland are one, have been for hundreds of years? Our interests are the same; we work together, play together, and, if need be, fight together. Every Scot worth the name thinks his country is the best and wants to do it credit, but we're not shedding any glory on Scotland when we're rude to a guest because she's English. When Marjorie comes back we must show her how kind and courteous Scots really are."

But Marjorie never came back. Perhaps the haunted cupboard was too much for her, perhaps she did not like the 'queer-like smell' from the linoleum factories, and thought the place dull and uninteresting.

Years later I spent an afternoon with her in her home in Surrey. She was large and handsome, and had several good-looking children. She said vaguely, "You know, I think I must have seen you when you were a small child. I once stayed a night in your house in Fife. You won't remember . . ."

I murmured something and changed the subject. I had not forgotten the lesson her visit taught us.

John once wrote, rather rudely,

"*I never likit the Kingdom of Fife*,"

and certainly we never loved it as we loved the Borders, but looking back our life there seems full of sunshine.

Some time ago we crossed the Forth Bridge, anxious to
see how much remained of the place we remembered so
well. We found practically nothing. The big Manse
garden had disappeared. The Manse itself was still there,
but crushed among tenements. Of our dear Hyacinth Den
not a vestige remained : electric trams clanged through
streets that had not existed in our day. It depressed us at
the moment, but, once away, the horrid reality faded, and
our memories remained.

Pathhead, where our father's church was, stood at the
top of the Path, a rather steep hill connecting our little
town with the much larger town of Kirkcaldy. At the
foot of the Path was the Harbour, a fascinating place where
foreign sailors might be met with strolling about in a
friendly way. They could sometimes be persuaded to let
us go on board their ships, and once a Norwegian captain
gave us coffee in gaily painted bowls.

The Path seemed to me a *very* long way from home (I
suppose it was about a quarter of a mile), and I was always
in dread of being caught in the middle of it by the Last
Day. I knew that dread Day would come suddenly—with
a shout. The angel Gabriel would stand with one foot
on solid ground—probably the linoleum factory—and one
foot on the sea, near the Inchkeith Light, I thought, and
blow a trumpet, whereupon the heavens would roll up like
a scroll. The only scroll I had ever seen was a brandy
scroll, made of treacle, which somehow added to the
horror. Another thing that worried me a good deal was
Eternity. I could more or less cope with no ending, but
no beginning was beyond me, and I simply had to rush
madly about the garden when the thought of it came into
my head.

There was nothing interesting or romantic about Pathhead except the sea and Ravenscraig Castle, once the home

of the ancient St. Clairs. We liked Sir Walter Scott's ballad of the 'lovely Rosabelle':

> "Each St. Clair was buried there,
>   With candle, with book, and with knell;
>   But the sea-caves rang and the wild winds sang
>   The dirge of lovely Rosabelle."

It is odd to think that time meant nothing to us in those days. So far as we were concerned the King still sat in Dunfermline town, calling for a 'skeely skipper' to sail his ship to 'Norraway over the faim,' and many a time we looked out to sea watching for the gallant ship that never more came home.

More even than the sea and the Harbour we loved the Coal-pit, and felt we were indeed greatly blessed to have one so near our home. There was no romance about the Coal-pit, but there were glorious opportunities to get thoroughly dirty. We had many friends among the miners, and they gave us rides on trolleys, and helped us to make see-saws, and admitted us into outhouses containing, among other treasures, the yellow grease that trains are greased with.

No wonder Mother and Ellie Robbie hated the Coal-pit. We escaped there at every opportunity and generally came back much the worse of wear. Willie broke his arm on one occasion, and I had the nails torn from one hand.

But it was John who had the really spectacular accident, and we younger ones felt defrauded that we only knew about it from hearsay. When he was about four years old he fell out of a carriage, and the back wheel caught his head, making a frightful wound. They were passing through a village at the time, and Mother used to tell us dramatically how she rushed into a cottage and without a by-your-leave began pulling out drawers to get something with which to cover it. It was nearly a year before John was able to be up and about again, but terrible as the experience was, it was worth it. He had been a delicate child, but after that he was as hardy as a Shetland pony.

I never heard anyone say we were either interesting or attractive children, but we were uncommonly wild and mischievous. Anyone who doubted the theory of Original Sin in Father's hearing was invited to regard his family. Sometimes we did really wicked things like celebrating a birthday by setting light to a pile of wood at the Coal-pit, and nearly burning the place down.

The Pathhead people said, " They're a' bad, but the lassie's the verra deil," so I can't claim to have been a refining influence. John, as eldest, was, of course the ringleader in all our escapades, and a funny little desperado he must have been. with his large head, the forehead crossed by a wide scar. In our rough play his head was always getting knocks, and the doctor warned him to be careful. So, when he fell from a height—as he frequently did, for he was fond of climbing—we would stand a bit away and shout, " Is it your scar ? ", prepared, if the answer was in the affirmative, to run and run, it mattered not where, so long as we did not see what happened next.

I never knew anyone with such a thirst for information as John. Long before it was time for him to begin regular lessons he had taught himself to read. Everything interested him and he tried to get information from everyone he met. At one time it was fowls, and he sat for hours with a specialist on the subject, returning home with pictures of prize cocks which he insisted on pinning round the nursery walls. For a long time it was ships, and he spent most of his time with a retired sea-captain. Next it was precious stones, and he accosted every lady, known to him or not, and asked her about the stones she was wearing.

John was an amazing contrast to his sisters and brothers. We never asked for information on any subject, for we wanted none. We were ignorant and unashamed.

But John's great passion was always for books. I remember when he discovered he could make words rhyme. His first effort, a poem on the Covenanters, so impressed the Superintendent of the Sunday School that he had it printed on a card and presented one to each scholar, an action that made us all feel rather shy and silly. It led to my first acquaintance with a critic. A big boy, fourteen perhaps, happened to remark as we walked up the road together, that the poem wasn't worth printing, whereupon I ran at him and kicked him savagely, sobbing loudly the while. It was not that I had any idea whether the verses were good or bad, but they were *John's* verses, and as such must be treated with respect.

One wet afternoon when someone was ill in the house, John was told to amuse Willie and me quietly. What he did was to give us each a pencil and sheet of paper, and tell us to write a poem on the Battle of Bannockburn. Then he left us, locking the door behind him. As he was always very much our big brother and we were accustomed to obey his decrees, we both tried our hardest, and Willie did manage two lines :

> " On the 23rd of June
> When the bold de Bohun—"

But not a vestige of an idea came to me, so the prize (a pennyworth of acid drops) went to Willie.

It seems to me looking back that money, or the lack of it, mattered oddly little in our home. It certainly mattered nothing to Father, who was almost provokingly otherwordly, and if it had not been for Mother's practical common sense we would certainly have crashed. She was well fitted to bear the burden. We were far from rich, indeed after the failure of the Glasgow Bank there was little more than my father's modest stipend, but so well did Mother manage that the house was run with every comfort.

My mother was essentially a home-maker. Hers was no patient enduring of the trivial round, the common task ; she frankly delighted in the work the different seasons brought, and made us enjoy them with her. Fruit-pulling in the sunny kitchen garden meant ' skimmings ' for tea (is there anyone so ignorant as not to know that ' skimmings ' is the froth from the fruit as it boils in the pan ? and has anyone been so cheated by life as to have missed eating strawberry-skimmings with freshly churned butter on a hot girdle scone ?). Autumn with its yellow leaves and shrill winds brought apples to be stored and plums to be ripened ; then it was December when the plum-pudding was mixed in a gigantic bowl and then divided into a number of smaller bowls, one or two for ourselves, the others to be given away, for Mother shared everything she had.

But the spring cleaning was the sweet of the year to her. She prided herself on being able to get the house cleaned meticulously with the minimum of discomfort to its inhabitants, and how she enjoyed it ! She began in the attics and worked down, superintending everything herself, glorying in letting the clear cold March sunlight into every corner.

There was one March that Mother never to the end of her days forgot—the March my little sister was born. As she grew old and frail she liked more and more to recall it. She would say, " I think perhaps that was the very happiest time of my life, those weeks after Violet came. Not that I hadn't always been happy, but the years before had been rather a mêlée. Now I had found my feet, more or less, and church work and housekeeping and baby-rearing no more appalled me. It was in March she was born. We had finished the spring-cleaning well before-hand, and the Deacon's Court had painted the staircase, and we had saved up for crimson stair and landing carpets, and the house was as fresh as it's possible for a house to be. I lay there with my baby, so utterly contented, listen-ing to your voices as you played in the garden in the spring sunshine, pleasant thoughts going through my head about my healthy, happy children, and thanking God for the best man ever woman had. It seems to me that my cup of happiness must have been lipping over then. . . ."

We were all glad about our baby sister. From the first she was a specially precious child. I had lived a tumbled, puppy-like life, giving and taking hard knocks, expecting no special consideration because of my sex, but with Violet the boys were never anything but gentle. Marget, always a stern critic of our failings (the only thing she could say in our favour was " There's one thing about our bairns, they're no' ill-kinded to beasts "), almost worshipped the child.

Marget was a great figure in our childhood. She was a large woman with a broad, plain face, and a most capacious and comfortable lap. I never remember any servant troubles in our house. Mother often said that her servants had been her best friends, and certainly they made all the difference to the peace and comfort of our home. A kitchen without Marget moving methodically about was unthinkable. We children were devoured with curiosity about her age, but she would never reveal it, exasperating us with quips such as " I'm as old as ma little finger and I'm older than ma teeth." We thought she was about eighty, but as a matter of fact she came to us before she was forty. It was her massive appearance that deceived us, and the sort of majestic caps she wore. When a certain aunt came to stay, to her was given the honour of creating a new cap. Bandboxes were brought down from the attics, bits of velvet ribbon and lace were chosen, and the whole household took an interest in the progress of the cap.

When Marget came to enquire about the place, away back in the beginning of time, she said, " I doubt you'll think my wage awful big—I've been getting £14 a year." When it was increased she had qualms of conscience that she was being overpaid, and insisted, " I dinna work for it except on washing days." As if any wage, however large, would have paid for her interest and loyalty !

John was always the favourite—but she felt it her duty to deal faithfully with him when he disappointed her. A friend of his, known as Sandy Hutch, had, in Marget's eyes, put himself outside the pale by riding his pony on the Sabbath day. She prophesied that he would go straight to the Ill Place. (After that I always regarded this boy with a fearful interest as one who was Lost.) Later, Marget included Sir Walter Scott in the same condemnation, because he had written ' novelles,' upon which John remarked, " If Sir Walter's there, and Sandy going, I wouldn't mind being there too."

" Wheesht, laddie, wheesht," said Marget solemnly, her face white, " remember it's *where the worm dieth not and the fire is not quenched.*"

Marget remained with us until she was nearing the age we had credited her with, and when she went it was as if a strong prop had been removed.

To children ' born beneath the shadow of a steeple ' life must always be a little different. Perhaps we were more aware than other children of the sound of ' time's wingéd chariots.' Brought up in the doctrine of John

Calvin we ought, I suppose, to have been full of repressions and inhibitions. When I read of the terrible consequences of such an upbringing, how the long dreary Sabbaths and enforced attendance at church have driven many to crime and others to atheism, I laugh—like Fish. (Fish was a loofah with a boot-button for an eye, and belonged to Willie. His was an unholy influence. When anyone did or said anything rather noble, Fish laughed.) Calvinism sat lightly on our shoulders. I think Father had too keen a sense of humour to be the stern Victorian parent. He was a very human saint, and never expected because he was virtuous that there should be no more cakes and ale. No one lived more simply, but if good things came his way he enjoyed them to the full. Desiring no possessions for himself, he was enthusiastic about the possessions of others. Jewels he loved. A jeweller's window was a feast to him, and he liked to quote to us, " And the twelve gates were twelve pearls ; every several gate was of one pearl, and the street of the city was pure gold, as it were transparent glass."

On one occasion one of us said pertly, " That's a Jew's idea of Heaven," and Father only said mildly, " Perhaps, but it's very beautiful. All the same I'd prefer a Border glen myself—' Bourhope at a reasonable rent,' as the old farmer said."

It was my father who taught us to love books. His study was a book-lined room, with a carpet of grey and scarlet checks (excellent for playing games) and a clock on the chimney-piece with the honestest face a clock could have. To that room we went every winter evening after tea, and Father either read to us or told us stories.

There we met ' Alice ' and went with her through the Looking-glass to Wonderland. We met Bully Bottom and his fellow actors, and the Knights of *Ivanhoe*. We thrilled to *The Long Pack*, and shouted with delight over the exploits of Tom Sawyer and Huckleberry Finn. We enjoyed an evening among the cunning fellows in Grimm, and felt vaguely uneasy in Hans Andersen's sad, lovely enchanted land, but what we liked best were the stories Father had heard from his mother, many of them unprinted and handed down by word of mouth. There was

> " The Red Etin of Ireland,
> Who lived in Ballygand,
> And stole the King's daughter,
> The King of fair Scotland."

And *The Bannock that went to see the World*, with its cynical ending, " We'll all be in the tod's hole in less than a hunner years," and many others.

But what of the Sabbath ? Was it really such a day of profound gloom as it has been pictured ? Not to us ; most certainly not to us. True, toys and story-books were put away, and we trotted to church both morning and afternoon, where our boredom was lightened by the gift of small pieces of liquorice, which we called ' black sugar,' from an elderly gentleman in the next pew. There was no porridge on Sunday morning, ham and eggs instead, and there was cake for tea, and sugar biscuits. After tea we played Bible games.

The Bible was a veritable mine of wealth to us, not, I fear, because it was the Word of Life, but because it was full of such grand stories. The Bible and the *Pilgrim's Progress* we never tired of, but what we could not bear was to have these broken down to us. Much of them we did not understand, but the roll and thunder of the words delighted us, and the drama.

We used to march round and round the nursery table blowing lustily on trumpets to cause the walls of Jericho to fall, or Walter, as Jeremiah, would be lowered by John

23

and Willie into the pit (which was the back of the old sofa) with ' clouts under his armpits,' or again, Willie and Walter, as spies, lay prostrate on the sofa (now the flat roof of an Eastern house) while I, as Rahab, the harlot, concealed them with flax. Shadrach, Meshach and Abednego in the fiery furnace was the most thrilling game of all, but it was stopped when we burned the nursery rug and nearly set the house on fire.

My own favourite was Jonathan and the honey. I always wept when Jonathan said, " I did but taste a little honey with the end of the rod that was in mine hand, and, lo, I must die," remembering that I had done many worse things than that without being put to death.

For an hour before bed-time we pored over ' bound books ' which contained serial stories that were considered Sabbath reading. They were mostly about men and women who had suffered for their faith, and from them we learned that courage and self-sacrifice were among the greatest things in life. But I fear that as I read of the horrors of the Inquisition, I often wondered why the poor victims had not tried saying their prayers in bed and so saved themselves such fiery trials.

Our Sabbath always ended with singing, each of us choosing his or her favourite psalm or hymn, and for a finish we all demanded ' Prophet Daniel.' It was a sort of chant. The first line ran : " Where is now the Prophet Daniel ? " This was repeated three times and the fourth line was the answer : " Safe in the Promised Land." The second verse told the details : " He went through the den of lions " (repeated three times) " Safe to the Promised Land." The great point about this hymn was that any favourite hero could be added at will. Of Sir William Wallace we sang, " He went up from an English scaffold," and we always insisted on adding Prince Charles Edward's name, defiantly assuring ourselves that the Prince who had come among his people seeking an earthly crown had attained to a heavenly one, and was safe in the Promised Land.

My father never seemed to mind about his children's wild ways, perhaps because his own past had not been blameless—we had heard whispers of a not very perfect boyhood—and he was never hard on us as long as we did not cheat or tell lies, or hurt anything weaker than ourselves. He was really amazingly patient, but it was never safe to presume too much on his mildness. One of the few times I ever saw him really angry, was when he was holding a class for young communicants in his study, and we crawled into the cubby-hole under the stairs which contained the meter, and *turned off the gas.*

Father emerged like a raging lion and caught poor Walter who had lingered. The rest of us had gained the attics and were in hiding.

Happy though we were in Fife, the thought of our two summer months in the Borders was never far from our minds. How often we talked of the journey, dwelling on every step of the way. First to Edinburgh, where we got lunch in a shop, then to Peebles, where we passed an hour or two in the old house on the bridge which had been Father's home in his boyhood, and where his brother and sisters still lived. Peebles seemed a sort of land of Canaan to us, flowing with milk and honey, which meant sweets in abundance, not one at a time but as many as we cared to eat, and toyshops where we were allowed to choose anything in reason. It was only twelve miles by rail from Peebles to Broughton—Mother's home—and every foot of the way was exciting. The tunnel so long and black that it seemed unlikely that we should ever emerge into the daylight, Tweed beside us most of the way, the thrill of guessing if a heron would be seen at the meeting of Tweed and Biggar Water. Every landmark was greeted with shouts, until we puffed importantly into a flowery station. The large board with Broughton painted on it seemed to us a most unnecessary thing. Surely there were no people living so ignorant as not to recognise Broughton when they saw it.

With glad yells we leapt from the train, all agog to meet our friends, the Station-master, the porter and the local worthies who were always there when a train came in. It was perhaps rather complacent of us to expect a welcome, for to most of the inhabitants our absence must have seemed good company. " Thae little deils o' Buchans back again ! "

Our grandfather's house, The Green, stood at the end of the village, a tall, white-washed building with a steep roof. At one time it had been an inn, and the rooms had still numbers painted on the doors. Our play-room was called *Jenny Berry*, but the reason of the name is lost in the mists of antiquity. The garret, which ran the length of the house, was called *Frizzel's End*. (John had a theory that Frizzel had been a highwayman and was done to death there.) We liked to go to the garret on wet days, and hear the heavy summer rain drum on the roof, and browse among the old books and magazines that were piled in one corner. There was *Oliver Twist* in green pasteboard covers and very small print, some years of *Blackwood's Magazine*, which meant endless good reading, and several bound volumes of *Punch* and *Good Words*.

We never tired of hearing Mother tell of her childhood in Broughton ; a whirl of excitement it must have been, we thought enviously, when we heard of Ord's Circus in the stackyard, peep-shows in the barn, and Hallowe'en held in the stone-flagged kitchen with all its rites. When she was sent to boarding-school at The Priory, Peebles, though it was only twelve miles away it seemed as far as Timbuctoo, and she wept with delight when her three brothers were brought down to see her.

Mother was at home for the summer holidays when she met Father, and they got engaged. Instead of going back to school she was sent to Edinburgh to take cooking-lessons and learn to be a good housekeeper. She was barely seventeen, and her hair was put up for the first time on her wedding-day.

We listened eagerly to every detail of that day, and felt it hard that we had not been there to smell the kitchen simmering with all the good things—hare soup, turbot, game, creams, and trifles. The guests had certainly not been starved, for, after luncheon and the speeches were over, they were regaled with tea. Our mouths watered as we heard of great rich cakes being cut down with a lavish hand, and the thick cakes of shortbread with sweeties on the top—just the things we liked most.

It had been a great storm that December, drifts were piled high round the house, a white bridal in very truth, and we who only knew Broughton in summer sighed at the thought of missing such a sight.

When Mother told us of the white satin gown and little square-toed kid slippers, with stiff rosettes and blue silk laces, she would sometimes say, " Ah well, I had my day." Willie, who was sensitive to the feelings of others, once assured her, " But, Mother, you'd do again."

The household at The Green consisted of our grand-parents, their three sons and their daughter, our kind and gentle aunt, called by us ' Antaggie.' She did not marry as long as her parents needed her and was there all through our childhood. My grandmother, whom we held in great respect and not a little awe, was a somewhat formidable old lady. A word of praise from her meant a lot to us :

the pity was we so seldom earned it. But ' Antaggie ' had a wonderful gift for seeing the best in us, for finding excuses for our worst behaviour, and for comforting us when the heavens were darkened. I can see her now on a hot summer day, in a blue dress and shady hat, patiently picking fruit in the garden, while we gambolled round her, pretending to help but really only stuffing ourselves with gooseberries : or seated at the piano, singing in a small sweet voice *Tam Glen* or *Robin Adair*. She once confided to us that her great ambition was to have a sealskin coat like the one our mother had when she was married ; and when she was free to marry the man she had long cared for, John remembered that wish, and sent her from South Africa (he had just gone out to be with Lord Milner) a cheque to buy it, and—what she prized even more— a letter telling her what she had meant to us through our childhood.

Our grandfather died when we were still children. For years he had suffered from asthma and was never able to do much, but sometimes he drove himself in a low basket trap to overlook the work in his outlying farms. We often accompanied him, and I remember how the fat white pony stopped of his own accord when we met anyone on the road, for he knew his master was friends with everyone and enjoyed nothing better than a ' crack ' with all anp sundry. One occasion when he came to our rescue is imprinted on my memory. We had got into trouble with the village blacksmith—not an unusual thing—but this time we thought we were suffering for righteousness' sake. He had shut up three young starlings in a cage and we took it upon ourselves to set them free. The 'smith had often threatened to horsewhip us, for we were constantly trespassing in his garden, chasing his ducks, and making a nuisance of ourselves generally, and here was his opportunity. Hiding behind the dyke we heard his roar of wrath when he discovered the empty cage, and fled down the burnside. The 'smith, only waiting to get his whip, followed us. We knew then what Jack the Giant Killer must have felt when the giant came after him, but we alas! had none of Jack's cunning and aplomb. All we could do was to climb a tree.

From our precarious perch—it was a small tree to bear four hefty children—we watched the approach of our enemy. He was telling the world what we would be like when he was finished with us. The fact that he was wearing the black leather apron of his trade seemed to make him more frightsome.

When he reached us and looked up, we saw that his eyes were red with rage, and, taking the trunk of the tree in his powerful hands, he began to shake it. That we had not expected. We clung desperately, twisting our legs round the branches, but in another minute we must have dropped like ripe fruit, had not an interruption occurred.

Unnoticed by us our grandfather had appeared on the scene. I shall always remember him as he stood there facing our fierce accuser, a frail figure in baggy tweeds and a panama hat that had seen many summers. In one hand he carried a copy of the *Spectator*, and anything more remote from heat and angry passions could hardly be imagined.

He nodded to the 'smith and said mildly, "Nothing wrong, I hope, Mr. Guthrie?" (That astonished us. Mr. Guthrie! We had not known that he had any name except 'the 'smith.')

"Wrong?" The word jerked out red-hot, and a list of our misdeeds followed. Grandfather listened in his courteous way, and then spoke. We could not hear what he said, but his tone was conciliatory, and gradually the 'smith began to look less turbulent, and in a short time we were told to come down.

Surprised at the turn things had taken we slithered to the ground, looking none the better for our sojourn in the tree.

Grandfather's voice was cold as he said, " I've promised Mr. Guthrie that after this you will respect his property and cease making a nuisance of yourselves ! "

We gaped, and the 'smith said, " Well, I'll be going."

" I'm sorry you were interrupted," Grandfather said. " Good-day to you, sir. Come along, children."

He walked on, and we followed considerably crestfallen, and feeling vaguely ashamed of ourselves without quite knowing why. (After all it was an act of mercy to let birds free.)

Before we reached home Grandfather turned and looked at us, and we were relieved to see that his face was kind again.

" Come down to tea looking less like tramps," he said, and then, " Johnny, how old are you now ? "

" Nearly thirteen."

" Don't you think it's about time you stopped leading the others into mischief ? Oh, I know, I know, you wanted to be kind to the birds, but I fear you wanted even more a chance to annoy the 'smith. Learn a little common sense. If I hadn't suspected something and turned up in time you might have got a pretty bad beating, but what would have been much worse, you might have got a decent, hard-working man into trouble. That I *would* have been sorry about. Run off now—and we won't worry your grandmother with this episode."

During our summers in the Borders there must have been dreary times, days when nothing seemed worth doing, days when we made ourselves miserable by quarrelling, days when we smarted under the feeling of being unjustly blamed—but the odd thing is I cannot remember them.

Always it seems :

> " The day was just a day to my mind,
> All sunny before and sunny behind. . . ."

Those halcyon mornings when we set out after breakfast each with a ' piece,' and spent long hours among the hills, eating ' blaeberries ' till our mouths were dyed purple, drinking from every burn we came to, racing on the hill-tops like mad things.

When John was at Oxford he got a book specially bound for me, a sort of commonplace book, and in it he wrote of those days :

> " We were two children, you and I,
> Unkempt,' unwatched, far-wandering, shy,
> Trudging from morn with easy load,
> While Faery lay adown the road . . .
> Sometimes, on sunny summer's noon,
> Our wearied feet got elfin shoon,
> And we toiled up the hill so high
> We seemed to knock against the sky,
> While far above the clouds we heard
> The singing of the snow-white Bird . . .
> You in such lore were wondrous wise,
> My princess of the shining eyes.
> Our favour was the crimson Rose,
> Our light the glow-worm's lamp, our ways
> The Road the King of Errin goes,
> And that is to the End of Days."

" Princess of the shining eyes " is good, but brotherly compliments were rare. When I provoked my brothers they had a hideous habit of chanting in unison some verses

---

[1] The word ' unkempt ' affronted Mother greatly. She said she was surprised that the next word was not ' unwashed.'

they had composed, enumerating all my worst points, and finishing :

> "If you want to see how ugly a girl can be,
> Come and look at she,
> Buchan Nan."

"Smells are surer than sights or sounds to make the heart-strings crack," and the smell of mint with the sun on it brings back to me a day that seemed the distilled essence of all summer days that have ever dawned. At the bend of the road leading to Broughton Place Glen (once the home of Mr. ' Evidence ' Murray) there used to stand an old mill, and above it a mill-pond, a very favourite haunt of ours. On this hot, still day the water for some reason had been drained off, and the sun had baked the mud fairly dry, so that it was possible for us to walk into the middle and inspect the water-hen's nest that we knew to be there. The flags were higher than our heads, and we walked in a green underworld that smelt deliciously of peppermint. I suppose the water-hen's nest must have been an old one, there were no eggs in it, but that did not damp us at all, and I, for one, was beatifically happy.

It was at the old mill that, wandering alone one day, I came across an artist. He nodded kindly, if vaguely, to me, and went on with his work, while I, encouraged by his smile, settled myself before him, hoping to be included in the picture. Still kind, he gave me sixpence to go away. I took it.

As we grew older our love for Broughton did not diminish, but increased as we realised what enchanted land it was. There was one place, at the foot of the loan between Broughton and Skirling, near the churchyard with its ruined Kirk, a huddle of stones that had once been a house, beside it a well, and round it some ancient twisted trees, which seemed to us a most eerie place. John used to stand and look at it, and tell us that at one time the village lay in the shadow of a great wood, a remnant of that forest where once Merlin harped and Arthur mustered his men. Years later he wrote a book about the church and the huddle of stones that had been the manse. In *Witch Wood* he told the story of the minister of Woodilee (Broughton), a tale of the days of Montrose, set against the background of an intolerant Church, and the pagan worship of an older Scotland.

It was a heart-breaking business every year when the time came to return to Fife. We really did suffer horribly. Tweed might almost have been in spate with the tears we shed. Next summer was much too far away to mean anything to us ; we were without hope. For days before our departure we went round saying good-bye to our favourite haunts. I kissed the calves and the kittens, stroked the horses and even patted the pigs. We glared with bitter envy at everybody to whom this Eden was home and who would never be driven out of it.

Our grandmother would remind us in bracing tones that our Fife home was a most desirable place, and that we had everything there that any child could want. We admitted it dully. Fife was all right, but—Broughton was our darling own place.

It was odd to live over again those partings with the next generation. Their love for the place was as keen as ours had been, their sorrow at leaving as despairing, and they were in a worse case for they had to go home to England.

"I'm not homesick, I'm Scotland-sick," one of them said, and when I asked him what he thought of most in Broughton when he was away from it, he said, " The creak of the gate at the level crossing." That summed it all up for him—a long happy day ended, the return home across the footbridge and through the creaking gate, supper to look forward to, a game by the fire, dreamless sleep, and another happy day tomorrow.

We were hopeless sentimentalists about the corner of the Borders that was particularly our own, and yet, when we had crossed the Firth of Forth and were once more in the Kingdom of Fife, we were conscious of a stirring of interest. The rabbits must have missed us, Lord Turkey would be glad to see us back, there might be a new kitten —and there was always the sea and the friendly Inchkeith Light.

One September when we returned to Fife we were aware of a certain disturbance in the home atmosphere. Father and Mother seemed to have much to talk about in private, and we were frequently shooed out of the study.

In time we heard from John that changes were brewing. Father had been, or was going to be, offered a church in Glasgow, and he and Mother were trying to make up their minds whether to go or stay. We could not see why there should be any hesitation; always to children 'changes are lichtsome,' and the thought of going to a city was full of charm. When at last the decision was made and the parents set off for Glasgow to look for a house, we stood on the doorstep and earnestly advised them to get one near a coal-pit.

It might be supposed that we would have shown regret at leaving a place full of kindly people, where we had been happy, but we did not because we felt none. Our time was taken up packing our small belongings, and leaping delightedly about in the dishevelled rooms. We did not even regret the garden, where so many of our happiest hours had been spent until we discovered the coarser delights of the Coal-pit. Part of the sunny garden had

34

been christened by John 'Nontland,' because it was ruled by one, Nont. He had once been a common nine-pin, but having had a hole bored through his middle by a red-hot wire he became possessed of a mystic power and personality.

Besides ourselves and Nont and two white Russian rabbits with pink eyes, there was only one other denizen of our Kingdom—a turkey with a broken leg, a lonely lovable fowl whom John out of pity had raised to the peerage and the office of Prime Minister. We would certainly have grieved over leaving the turkey and the rabbits, but, as it happened, we did not have to leave them. Lord Turkey died suddenly, and a wicked weasel got in and sucked the blood of the rabbits. The blank they left was great, and we so hated the sight of the empty hutch that we felt the sooner we were away the better.

Nont, it was obvious, could not be left to aliens who would not recognise his Kingliness, so we decided to give him a funeral pyre. John said it was 'suttee.' We accepted this as we accepted all John's statements, but we learned later that he had got his facts mixed. Anyway, with a great crackle of twigs and the smell of burning leaves Nont left the world.

Pathhead was a hospitable place, and in winter we had many parties—simple affairs; a large tea followed by games, and finishing at an early hour with jam-tartlets and lemonade. But just before we left we were bidden to our first real party, quite a pretentious one, beginning at six and going on till eleven. John wore his Eton suit and a very wide collar and was instructed never to lose sight of me. I must have been about eight at the time, and very proud of the fact that I had golden butterflies on my slippers.

It seemed to us a very large house. A maid took me upstairs, while John was directed to leave his coat in a cloak-room.

There were a lot of girls taking off their wraps in the bedroom, all alarmingly grown-up, all laughing together.

The maid, a kindly creature, removed my cloak and brushed my hair, and then, giving me a little shove, remarked, " There now," and left me. I was too shy to do anything but stand where I was. No one paid any attention to me, and when at last the room was empty I crept cautiously to the door and looked out. To my profound relief there was my faithful John, and with him another brother and sister well known to us, often, indeed, our companions in crime—Dan and Annie. Like us, they were feeling rather oppressed by the occasion.

We looked down into the hall and saw that already some of the company were dancing, dancing in a correct, grown-up way quite beyond us.

What a party ! What were we to do till nine o'clock when Ellie Robbie would come for us ?

We stood about for what seemed a long time, and then a half-open door attracted Dan's attention and he looked in.

" It's their bathroom," he announced, and we all had a look. We had never seen such a bathroom, so large, and so full of gadgets. John at once began to investigate, and under his direction we were soon engaged in an exciting game of pirates, first taking the precaution to lock the door.

There was simply no end to the things we could play at in that bathroom, and we had a thoroughly enjoyable time. The *Little Revenge* had just gone down to be lost evermore in the main, when John took out his Waterbury watch and after some intricate calculations said it was nearly nine o'clock.

Annie got her own cloak and mine, and we all slipped quietly downstairs, wet, but in excellent spirits. The hall was empty except for Ellie Robbie and a maid, but through a door we could hear sounds of talk and laughter.

When we reached home Mother could not understand what sort of party it had been. Had we enjoyed the supper? There was no supper, we told her; we hadn't had anything to eat. All we could do was to babble about a bathroom where water squirted out of the ceiling when we pulled a cord, and hit us like a wave of the sea from all sides when we turned a handle. Later she learned from the mother of Dan and Annie how we had spent the evening, and reproached John for having behaved in such a rude and childish manner. I was honestly astonished to hear that we had done anything wrong. You went to a party to enjoy yourself, didn't you? And we had certainly done that.

In the end of November we left Fife. John was thirteen, and Baby Violet eight months.

Mother was very sad when it came to parting with so many trusted friends, and I remember one of the oldest and kindest saying to her :

" My dear, you're vexed to go, and I'm glad you're vexed to leave us, but you're taking all your own with you. You don't know what it means to leave a grave."

We wondered what she meant. Why should we leave a grave? When Marget tried to make us say "If I'm spared" after any statement about what we meant to do, we would reply, " But, Marget, we're *always* spared."

CHAPTER II

"As we came in by Glasgow-town."
Old Ballad.

THE month of November is hardly the best time to make acquaintance with the city of Glasgow, and I have heard my mother say that we were just given time to get our goods and chattels under cover when the rain descended and the floods came and went on for weeks.

Children are indifferent to weather, but I remember thinking that Glasgow was surely a very dark place.

While the 'flitting' was being accomplished the three boys went to Broughton, but I begged so hard to go with the furniture that Mother gave in. She thought I wanted to be the first to see our new home, but what I really wanted was to attend the Induction Soirée. I had no idea what that was, but I was convinced in my own mind that it would be of thrilling interest and more than oriental splendour.

When I found that it was only tea and buns and dull speeches, it was borne in on me that I had played Esau's part, and I thought rather bitterly of my brothers at Broughton. But I did have the ride in a cab through lighted streets, and saw dead rabbits hung up outside a butcher's shop, a sight never seen in Pathhead.

The boys came home full of travellers' tales. Broughton in winter had quite come up to their expectations. They had been allowed to work the machine that cuts up turnips for the sheep ; they had ridden a new pony called Sulky ; Grandfather had given each of them a new shilling, and 'Antaggie' had prepared 'a feast' for them every day. (A 'feast' consisted of a selection of sweets and some grapes or an orange.) Fortunately no one remembered to ask what the Induction Soireé had been like.

The boys at once explored the house from garret to cellars. It was a good house, square with fair-sized rooms, and—what specially pleased Father—a well-placed staircase with shallow steps. What intrigued my brothers was the basement. They found there what I had failed to notice, a door with Dark Room painted on it, and that was enough for many wild surmises. It was a Nihilists' Lair, a Robber's Cave, a Murderer's Den, so we pretended to believe, but we knew at the back of our minds that Father was right, and it was nothing worse than the place where the former owner of the house had developed his own photographs.

In Queen Mary Avenue—called, I suppose, for the ill-fated Queen who had lost everything near here at the Battle of Langside—it was difficult to believe that we were only about two miles from a great city. It was a quiet road, shaded with trees, and each of the solid grey houses stood in a large garden.

We were indeed lucky to have a garden. We might have had to live in a tall house in a street or even in a flat, and have had no place to work off our superfluous energy. As it was, we had trees to climb, and a selection of high walls, and at the bottom of the garden there was a large and dilapidated green-house with nothing in it but a passion-flower which must have been immortal to survive the usage it got. Shelves empty of plants rose in tiers and made a perfect stage for a sea-fight, and a broken telescope found in the Dark Room added verisimilitude to the scene. We took turns of being Nelson clapping the glass to his sightless eye.

In one of John's earliest books—*Scholar-Gipsies*—he describes our garden, in an essay called " Urban Greenery " :

39

" . . . The wall that circles the domain is of bricks, old, dim, and dirty. . . . Two valiant elms guard the corners, and midway a herd of little ashes and lindens form a thin grove, beneath which pale valley-lilies raise their heads in spring. What else is there? A privet-hedge, a lawn with wide borders of flowers, a minute shrubbery, two great beds by the house wall flanked by two birch trees, and little more. It is a place ' shorn and parcell'd,' with just enough magnitude to give point to its littleness.

" This urban garden is not without its association and fragments of past history. By the side over the young trees there rises an old square house, ivy-clad, with crowstep gables. This was once the manor-house of the place, when the suburb was still a smiling village among cornfields. There dwelt Woodrow, the historian of the Scottish Church, a man full of absurdity and kindliness, whose books are a charming farrago of gossip and grave reflection. One can fancy him walking here, composing his letters to Cotton Mather, and asking if the wild men and beasts of which his correspondent complained could be worse than the ravening Prelatists and lukewarm professors in his own unhappy country of Scotland. Over this place, too, was fought a great battle, which brought to the ill-fated Queen of Scots the loss at once of her kingdom and her liberty. Not half a mile off, fragments of steel are found to testify to the struggle, and in this very garden was once dug up a little cannon-ball of the kind used at the time, with the crust of three hundred years upon it. There is indeed a sort of faded gentility about all things here, a flavour of old wars and devilry, old godliness and peace."

This urban garden was a delight to Father, and made up to him for much that he missed in the city.

After thirteen years in Pathhead, with fields and woods almost at his door, homely little houses to visit, and never far out of sight of the tumbled waters of the Forth and the Inchkeith Lighthouse, it was hard to get accustomed to tramping endless dreary streets and climbing the stairs of high tenements. The squalor and the misery he met with often sent him home sad at heart. But his garden always comforted him. He kept it entirely himself, and felt it a tonic for mind and body. To see Father in his garden was to see someone absolutely at peace with the world, but perhaps his happiest time was June, when the flowers he had coaxed to grow were in bloom, and when he could gaze to his heart's content at his beloved crimson hawthorn.

Father had never, alas ! been able to instil in the four of us any passion for gardening, but in Violet he found a kindred spirit. The tall man and the little child would go round hand-in-hand, greeting every flower, talking to them —as you would talk to a friend.

When we arrived in Glasgow we were not given any time to get into mischief. After hearing about the different schools, Father decided to send John to Hutcheson's Grammar School. It was within walking distance of our home, which was an advantage, and he liked the sound of it. For one thing it had a long record, having been founded in 1641 by one George Hutcheson and his brother Thomas as a hospital and school. It had continued through the centuries, and was now a grammar school under the Hutcheson Trust.

Willie and Walter and I became pupils at a little school with the high-sounding name of Queen's Park Academy and presided over by Mr. Moses Park. He taught the older children downstairs, we younger ones sat on low forms in an upper chamber, where Miss Marshall worked hard to get some ideas into our heads. Her younger sister, Miss Eliza, tried to teach me the piano, but, as

I had no ear for music and neither knew nor cared when I played wrong notes, it was a heart-breaking task for her. She was pretty, I remember, and sweet. I hope I did not age her before her time. The only encounter I remember having with Mr. Moses Park was one morning when he was giving us a Bible lesson. He fixed me with a stern eye and asked me to name anyone I knew who was a servant of God. I replied firmly that I did not know any, whereupon he made me come out to the middle of the floor and shake him by the hand.

"Now," he said, "you can say you have shaken hands with a servant of God."

I was not only shamed by this publicity but very sceptical about the statement. I knew all about servants of God, they had long white beards and tables of stone and brazen serpents, not in the least like our nice cheery-faced Mr. Park.

We liked Queen's Park Academy and the teachers and the pupils. (Marjorie Gullan, of verse-speaking fame, and her brother, Campbell Gullan, the actor, also children of the manse, were our fellow-pupils.) But life at that time was darkened for me owing to Mother making me wear a pinafore. She said all little girls wore pinafores, but the other girls at our school had tidy dresses, and their hair tied neatly back with a ribbon, while I had to flop about in a loose pinafore, with my curls completely untrammelled. Mother might have remembered that it is torture to a child to be different in the slightest degree from her contemporaries, but I expect she was too busy to give any thought to my whims. It was no light task to come to a strange place and have to begin at once to know everyone in a congregation, as well as get a household into proper order, and look after four wild children and a tiny baby. And Ellie Robbie was not there to help, having married a joiner. We had a nursemaid for Violet, very young and

42

completely inexperienced, but 'terrible bold and firm.' We brought her with us from Fife, and she never lost her salt-sea touch. When trout were brought in she called them 'thae herring,' and her voice sounded shrill compared with the soft Glasgow tones.

Believing that we should do in Rome as the Romans, Willie, Walter, and I at once acquired a rich Glasgow accent of which we were very proud. Father, however, did not admire it, so we kept it for school and spoke at home as we had always done.

Father's church was called John Knox Church, rather a fine building near the Clyde. It had been a fashionable locality in the days when Paisley Road was lined with the gardens of prosperous business men who had built villas there, when Kelvinside as a suburb did not exist, and Blythswood Square was considered well on to the Highlands. When we knew it, it was rather a dreary place, and all who could afford it were acquiring new houses or flats in outlying suburbs, so that the churches in the centre of the city were growing every year emptier and emptier. To keep them going at all meant hard and unceasing toil for the ministers. In one way Knox's was fortunate. The old minister, Ralph Smith, to whom Father was appointed colleague and successor, was a wealthy man and a very generous one, and he loved his church. He was not so very old when first we became acquainted with him, but owing to some ailment he could only walk with the aid of an arm and a stick, and even then with difficulty. He had a place in Lanarkshire, and came to preach at long intervals. I suppose Mr. Smith was what is called 'narrow,' certainly he would never have sung a hymn, and he believed in the Bible as it stood.

> "No sophistries could make him see
> Its slender credit."

But he was not, as many who hold fast to the past are, bitter and prejudiced. He was full of gentle charity, only to the Higher Critics did he feel bitterness. We children loved him from the first. He was never facetious with us, so we were always at our ease with him. I remember some of his wise words even now. When John told him he meant to go into Parliament, he said, " Look higher than the Woolsack, John," and he once laid his large soft hand on my unruly head and gave me the best advice he knew, " Take Jesus, Anna."

Mr. Smith could not have got a more considerate and understanding colleague than my father. He, too, loved old ways (though he knew it was not possible to keep things standing), and he introduced as few ' innovations ' as possible. The service had to be brought into line with present-day ideas, and the old precentor, who for long had raised the tune, had to give place to an organist and choir. Mr. Smith never mentioned the subject, but, when a hymn was given out, he sang a psalm. No one, I expect, noticed, except one little pitcher with long ears who stood beside him in the pew. It was hard for the old people—most of them Highland and very conservative—to like the new ways.

The first time we sang the children's hymn—

> " There is a happy land,
> Far, far away,"

an old elder stamped out of the church. When the choir was going to produce a cantata, an old woman, whom Father happened to be visiting, said bitterly, " I hear there's going to be a *comedy* in Knox's tonight."

" More like a tragedy," said poor Father, who hated the dismal things.

Happily for us Father never preached long sermons.

44

He had no paper, not even a note, which made what he said infinitely more impressive, and he spoke so urgently, as a dying man to dying men, that no one's attention wandered. He had a singularly beautiful voice, and when he stretched out both arms in the Geneva gown and gave the Benediction, " *May the peace of God, which passeth all understanding, keep your hearts and minds,*" we really felt that we had been blessed.

Knox's congregation came from all parts of the city, ' from Maryhill to Pollokshaws, from Govan to Parkhead,' and most of the people seemed to live on the top flat of the highest tenements, so Father had many a weary trek. It is not easy work to build up a congregation that has dwindled away. True, the people who were left were ' *stone and lime* ' people and could be depended on always, but new blood was badly needed and gradually it came. It was hard work for both our parents, but it was repaying work and their hearts were in it.

It is odd to remember that we regarded Mother—who must have been then just over thirty—as perilously old. We sometimes got quite worked up after she had been round saying goodnight, that she couldn't live much longer, and then what would we do? There was no end to Mother's activities. Most women find a house and family quite enough to keep them busy, but besides visiting constantly in the congregation she started a Women's Meeting which met every Monday, and took over a Bible Class for older girls on Sunday evening. Generally she spoke herself, but one evening, I remember, a man came to speak. He had a long mild face like a sheep, and he took as his subject, Jezebel. He wagged his head at us warningly and said, " Oh girrls, girrls, Jezebel was a bad one, girrls."

I thought of Jezebel, painting her face and tiring her

45

head and looking out of the window, asking Jehu in dulcet tones, " Had Zimri peace who slew his master ? " She probably deserved her end, but it seemed to me hard that she should still be held up as an awful example.

Speaking in public was always a terror to Mother, which made the work rather a strain. When I grew old enough to help, I could sympathise with her. Sometimes Mother was not present, and then I had to open the meeting with prayer. That was a great ordeal, and too much to ask of a young girl. I was so apt to forget everything I had meant to say that I got into a way of speaking in a very low voice so that nobody would know whether I had stuck or not. This amused my brothers, and they asked if I didn't mind God knowing I had stuck. Of course I didn't. After all, it is to be supposed God knew what I was trying to say.

On school days in winter we never saw each other in daylight. We went off after an early breakfast and did not return till the lights were lit. The day always began with prayers. Father, as he read the Bible (it was always the Old Testament in the morning), used to put an arm round the youngest so that she would not run about and make the rest of us laugh. Now I never read Christ's words to Jerusalem, " How often would I have gathered thee," without seeing that encircling arm.

After a couple of years at Queen's Park Academy, Willie and Walter joined John at Hutcheson's, and I was sent to the corresponding school for girls. John gained a scholarship in his first year, and the other two did quite well also, but—with shame I confess it—I was the dunce of the family.

It was not so bad in a little private school where nothing much was expected of one, but in a big school, one of a crowd, I simply sank to the bottom. Algebra and Mathematics I *could not* understand ; any but the simplest of sums left me helpless. Besides being naturally stupid, I must also have been careless and inattentive, not listening unless I was interested, and when exams came my sins found me out. Once I had to draw a map of Australia, and I made a sort of fret-saw outline which might have been anything ; some nameless ' hairy oobits ' stood for mountains ; Sydney and Melbourne, the only two towns I remembered, I put one at the top and the other at the bottom, and New Zealand I joined to Australia as a small excrescence. This achievement was sent to my father to see what he thought of his daughter's work. He did not say much, merely drew his hand over his mouth in a way he had, and asked what was to be expected of a girl who couldn't read Scott. Mother said briskly that she was ashamed of me, and recalled that she had once got a prize for Geography, while my brothers, hooting with laughter, congratulated me on my effort.

My ignorance was certainly not the fault of my English teacher, Miss Flora Sharp, who was a most efficient instructor of youth. She did not, however, suffer fools gladly, and had the sense to see that if a child sets herself not to learn it is labour lost trying to teach her. I can see her now, with her iron-grey fringe and piled-up hair and rigidly neat figure, eyeing me sardonically as I sat resisting education. Years later when I happened to be lecturing in Glasgow. I was aware of something vaguely familiar in a front seat. It was Miss Sharp, still smiling sardonically.

With school-work and play-time the winters passed and spring came, and always at the end of June we escaped to Broughton—more loved and sighed for than ever, now that we had become city-dwellers. One May we got a great and unexpected treat because of Walter. After being over-heated at football he had stood in a biting east wind and, as a consequence, went down with pneumonia. In a few weeks he was able to be up and to consume enormous meals. So many eggs did he devour that John told him he would never be able to look a hen in the face again, and drew a series of pictures portraying him turning gradually into an egg.

When he was well enough we all went for a month to the Island of Arran. Nothing could really spoil Arran, most lovely of islands, but in those days it was a paradise —only a very few houses, a handful of people, and complete freedom. There was a boat belonging to the house we had, and we spent most of our time in it, rowing out to get into the wash of the steamers, when we whummelled violently, in imminent danger of being capsized and drowned. One day in the midst of a furious altercation in the boat, Walter (so recently an invalid) fell into the sea and was rescued with difficulty. We took him home with the water from his clothes making pools at every step, and fled again seawards when we heard the lamentation with which Mother and Marget received him.

We met in Arran a race of people very different from the folk of Fife or our friends in the Borders. They spoke Gaelic among themselves, and to 'the visitors' a curious soft English with a lilt in it, rather like the Welsh.

One summer when we took a little house under Goatfell we had so many visitors that we were crowded out, and the boys and their friends had to sleep in a cottage belonging to our landlady, Mrs. Currie. This cottage had a byre containing a cow attached to it, and the walls were so thin that every movement of the cow was heard. The first morning when we asked how they had slept they said, "Oh, well, you see, the cow had a restless night."

Mrs. Currie belonged to an earlier and grimmer age. Father rather applauded her rigid notions, but we did not feel that they added to the joy of life. For fear of hurting

Mrs. Currie's feelings we were not allowed to bathe on Sunday mornings, and as a bathroom was the last thing you expected to find in an Arran house in those days, it was a real deprivation. When the hymn was given out in church, " O day of rest and gladness," we thought " O day of dirt and sadness." Mrs. Currie supplied us with milk as usual on Sundays but refused to take payment for it, and her husband shaved on Saturday night that he might use ' no edged tool ' on the Sabbath day.

We sometimes used to listen as we passed their cottage and heard her reading aloud from the Bible awesome things like " I have said to corruption, Thou art my father : to the worm, Thou art my mother and my sister." It made us shiver to hear her.

Another summer, some years after we had left Fife, we spent September in Dysart, about three miles from our old home in Pathhead. Mother had taken the house without seeing it, and was surprised to find that the owner had left not only her cat—named Gentle Annie—but also a clocking-hen under one of the beds. It really was a delightful house (had it been clean), right down on the sea-front, looking into the harbour. When the tide was high, we looked on nothing but water, and in the distance, my old friend the Inchkeith Light. The living-room, a long low room, had four windows. (This house was the original of the Harbour House in *The Proper Place*.) We felt it almost disloyal to Broughton, to enjoy so much being back on the Fife Coast, but it was such fun to race over the firm sand and see the salmon-cobles drawn up on the beach, to fish for ' poddleys ' off the rocks. It was fine, too, to meet the old friends and to be invited to parties and fêted, our faulty tattered past forgotten.

Nowhere are more loyal friends to be found than in the Kingdom of Fife. Going back to some function in the

Pathhead Church, some years after Father's death and nearly thirty years after he had been minister there, Mother and I were amazed and touched to find how many people still remembered him with gratitude and affection. One old elder came up to us and said : " Ye would mebbe no' hear that I'd lost ma wife ? Ay, she slippit awa mair than a year syne. Her last thought was that Mr. Buchan would gie her a welcome ower yonder." As we drove away Mother said with deep conviction in her voice, " Surely a minister's job is the most repaying on this earth."

CHAPTER III

" Ere my heart beats too coldly and faintly
To remember sad things yet be gay
I would sing a brief song of the world's little children
Magic hath stolen away."*

WALTER DE LA MARE.

VIOLET

A T first Violet was merely a new possession, one so small and weak and infinitely precious that we hardly dared to touch her. Later she became the most entrancing of playthings. We sat on the nursery floor when she was being bathed, laughing at the faces she made when she tasted soapy water on the sponge, playing the clown to make her chuckle. Her first attempts at walking and talking excited and thrilled us, but it was not until she was old enough to be a companion that I realised what it meant to have a sister.

Though she was so much younger than I was, I found that we spoke the same language, liked the same things, and were contentedly happy in each other's company. Up to this time I had asked nothing better than to be allowed to play wild games with the boys, but now I gladly gave up hours to take Violet out. It was my delight on a summer afternoon to brush her hair till it shone—I was proud of her beauty—and dress her in a fresh white frock and a little blue cloak that was the colour of her eyes, and, holding her hand tightly in mine, set off for a walk. The Queen's Park was quite near our house and was always suggested to us as the nicest place to walk, but what we found much more alluring was a wide street of shops leading up to the Park, called Victoria Road.

The boys would never look into shop-windows unless

there were books to see, or mechanical toys, or guns and fishing-tackle, but Violet would stand contentedly beside me as long as I pleased, to study the wares offered for sale.

It was our game to choose what hats we liked best, what dresses, coats, and shoes, and when that palled she would say, "Now go on with our story."

It was a story without beginning or end, added to every time we were alone together, all about what we would do 'some day.' We were going to live, Violet and I, in a vague place, very much like Broughton but with the sea as well as hills and moors, in a very small cottage, and sleep together in a box-bed in the kitchen. It had always been my dream to do that. As I looked wistfully into cottages I thought how snug it must be to sleep in the kitchen, with people all about, drinking tea and talking; no loneliness, no long passages between you and other friendly humans. And we were going to carry our babies as we had seen the village women do, with a plaid wrapped round both the mother and baby.

We expected to have a very busy life, baking and cooking and making jam, and scraping our pots on a flat stone by the burnside, sluicing them clean in a pool. The boys were going to be quite near, in another cottage, and we meant to ask them to meals and give them the things we liked best—roast chicken and cutlets, apple tart and trifle, and toasted cheese for tea.

We often got so excited about this blissful future that we forgot where we were and bumped into passers-by, who must have wondered what made us so 'hiloarious.'

On occasion Willie and Walter were not above listening to this family chronicle and contributing to it, though they always preferred the tales John told them, yarns of breathless adventure.

Violet was a good player and loved to be admitted to

the less violent of our games, but we were at school all day and she might have been rather lonely had it not been for another small girl, Bessie Jackson by name, who lived in a large house further up the avenue.

Never were two children less alike, but in spite of that —or because of it—they were great friends.

Bessie was a tough child. She had no use for fairy-tales or any such nonsense (" Is it true ? " she would ask, " well then "), but was interested in all practical things. No one could bring more verisimilitude into ' playing houses,' or bring up a family of dolls. Once, buried in a chair with a book, I watched the couple. Violet had been told to get a bed ready for two dolls, ill of some mysterious disease known only to Bessie, and was shaking up pillows and smoothing blankets, while Bessie undressed a patient expertly, discoursing the while about her father's business.

" My Pa has three big shops. Has your father a shop ? "

" No," said Violet regretfully—a shop would have been such fun ; " he preaches in a church."

" What about ? "

Reluctantly Violet confessed that she did not know.

" Our church is a long way, but Mother says when I'm five I'll go like all the others. You're past five, Bessie ; I expect you go to church."

" Not me," said Bessie, turning over the doll and addressing it, " Crying, are you, Muriel ? You've much need to cry—bringing 'fectious disease into my nursery. The whole lot of you'll be down with it tomorrow I wouldn't wonder, and me just beginning the spring cleaning.—How could I go to church, Vi ? Sunday's Pa's day at home. People come and we go places."

" But," Violet objected, " Sunday's the day you get Bible lessons and learn who made you."

53

" Nobody made me," said Bessie in loud, boastful tones. " Pa says I came from the shop. Well, who did make me then ? "

" God," said Violet solemnly.

" Now you're swearing, Vi Buchan," said Bessie, return-ing to her troublesome nursery, while poor Violet regarded her helplessly.

Violet knew all Father's fairy-tales, Hans Andersen and Grimm, George Macdonald, besides his own special ones, and she had a fairy of her own—Whuppity Stourie, who lived in the study chimney. It was this fairy's lovable habit to send small presents once a week or so to her friend, and Willie, Walter and I spent a good deal of time searching in little shops for things within reach of our small means, to tie into parcels as presents from Whuppity.

They were placed one at a time, generally on a Saturday, on the fender-stool, and Violet, who was on the watch, would tiptoe in, looking half-scared, half-jubilant, grab the parcel and, with a gasped-out " Thank you, Whuppity," would rush off to show it to Mother.

One morning she came down to find the study in dis-order—dust sheets over the furniture and a sweep hooting up the chimney. She ran with a stricken face to Marget, crying that the sweeps were in the study chimney.

" And what for no ? " Marget asked bracingly. " Ye're ower big to be feared for sweeps."

" But, Marget, you forget. I've a friend up there."

Violet was not comforted until evening, when a note was found from Whuppity, saying he was glad to have his house spring-cleaned. Then all was well.

To outsiders Violet seemed rather an unapproachable child. She hated to be kissed by strangers, and did not respond to blandishments, and was sometimes devastatingly honest in her replies. When some people whose very charming place she had visited on a wet day asked her expectantly what she had seen there, she said, " Rain." But to her own family she was passionately loving. On winter evenings when the time came near for our return from school, she would watch the tea being laid, the fire brought to a blaze, the curtains drawn, with a radiant face, and when the door was shut and we were all seated round the table she would give a deep satisfied sigh, and say, " I do like my own people." All family festivals, birthdays, Hallowe'en, and Christmas were times of extraordinary happiness to the child.

Her fourth Christmas was a particularly joyous season. She seemed positively transported with happiness, watching the parcels arrive, helping Father to cut holly and ivy and decorate the house, trotting after Mother, as she put out the extra silver and china that would be used, and trying to imagine what Santa would bring to her.

Mother was pleased to have a daughter who cared for dolls (I had never been worthy of a good doll), and was sitting late every night dressing two for her—a golden-haired beauty and a baby in long clothes. After much searching I had found in an obscure little shop a doll's feeding-bottle, and was looking forward eagerly to Vi's delight.

We had no Christmas-tree, but in the early morning we had the excitement of our stockings, at breakfast the cards and parcels that had been arriving for days, our Christmas dinner in the middle of the day and, after tea, Mother dressed like Santa Claus came in laden with presents. As the youngest, Violet was called up first, and her awe-struck face was a study, as she came forward timidly, but when she saw the dolls she forgot everything else. Her arms went out to clasp them, and with a hurried, fervent " Thank you, thank you, Santa," she retired to a corner with her precious burdens, with no thought of anything else in Santa's pack.

When we were all examining our presents, there was a sudden wail from Violet. " Santa's forgotten his gloves," and there lay two shabby leather gloves. " His hands will be so cold ! " she lamented.

Even to comfort her not one of us would have cast a shadow of doubt on her belief that the real Santa Claus had paid us a visit.

Father said, " I'll see that the owner gets them, Vi," and no one had a better right to them.

That was Violet's last Christmas. She died, the beloved child, three months after her fifth birthday. Died at Broughton—the place that we had fondly believed could cure all earthly ills—as the dawn was breaking on a perfect June day.

CHAPTER IV

" In a Conspicuous Town she lived."
Pet Marjorie.

PERHAPS nothing was ever quite the same after Violet's death, certainly not to her parents : nor to poor Marget.

One afternoon when she brought in the letters, she threw them on the table, salver and all, and said bitterly, " News frae a'body, but nane frae *her*," and wept into her apron.

Life changed for me in the autumn of that year when I went away to school : only to Edinburgh, for Mother wanted to have me as near home as possible, and not to a boarding-school, but to old family friends—the Norman Walkers.

Dr. Walker had been minister in Dysart when my father was in Pathhead, and he and his wife were always welcome guests at our manse. He was Editor of the *Free Church Record*, a scholarly man, with a witty, sarcastic tongue : his wife was highly original and amusing. Theirs was a delightful house to live in, for all sorts of interesting people came to it, and it was full of books.

Dr. Walker (' the D.D.' his wife called him) liked to be amused, so I learned always to have an answer ready and as a consequence became regrettably pert. When I went home it took the combined efforts of my three brothers to reduce me to order.

Mrs. Walker was a continual diversion. Immediately after breakfast she would summon me to ' classify ' the dishes. " Always try to make things as easy as you can for the servants " was her motto, and we put the knives

57

(tidily wiped with paper) together, the cups and saucers and plates in neat piles. Then we saw that the marmalade dish was ready for next morning's breakfast, and got fresh jam and butter for the tea. My bedroom had to be left scrupulously neat every morning, all the things pulled off to air the bed, night things folded, hot-water bag emptied.

"You would never ask a maid to go into an unaired room with everything lying about, would you ? " she would say and supplied the answer herself, " No, you would be ashamed."

Continually busy with self-invented jobs, she regarded reading as rather a waste of time, but she saw to it that the flood of reading matter that came to the house was put to good use. The American picture-papers were carried to mothers who had sons in the States ; invalids were kept supplied with suitable reading, and all the highly-coloured adventure books were put aside for boys. One pile of pleasant happy-ending stories she described as ' capital for a confinement.'

She was a wonderful trainer, her husband being her one failure.

" I've been married to the D.D. for over forty years, and I haven't yet got him into the habit of folding back the rug when he goes to bed."

Dr. Walker regarded his wife with amused admiration.

" Kik, my dear," he would say, " where is the book I was reading before tea ? "

" Seek and ye shall find," was the answer, " not *speak* and she shall find. The book's lying where you laid it down."

She always sang as she marched about the house, generally jingling hymns, like :

> " ' I should like to die,' said Willie,
> ' If my Papa could die too ;
> But he says he isn't ready
> 'Cos he's got so much to do.' "

Or :

> " Did you ever put a penny
> In a missionary box ?
> A penny that you might have gone
> And spent like other folks."

When we went out together, it was my duty to see that she had not tied her veil so tightly as to crush her nose to one side. She rarely looked in a mirror, or cared what she wore, remarking that she had never been anything but plain. Plain she was, but there was something both interesting and attractive in her little blunt face. At sixty-odd she was almost as small and light as a child. She liked to sit with one foot under her, curled up in a corner of a sofa, with a bit of knitting in her hand, and tell the saga of her life to me, an absorbed listener, in the other corner.

Her sisters had married in India, one a soldier, the other an Indian civilian, and their children had been sent to their aunt in Dysart to bring up with her own. I cannot imagine a better person to bring up children. Life to her was so teeming with interest that no one could be bored and listless in her company. She had no use for a child who said :

" What'll I do next ? "

She believed in children finding their own ploys, but saw that they had plenty material to work on.

I particularly liked her stories of the escapades of her nephews Frank and Pat. She would finish :

" To think that Pat's now a knight and poor Frank in a grave in the desert."

There was a military touch about Mrs. Walker herself.

" Mustard to mutton," she would say. " Child, you would be dismissed the Mess."

59

Sometimes she told me of the changes she had seen in her life ; old families decaying, new ones rising up.

"You remember the Langtons ? No, I daresay not ; your mother would know them. They were plain people who rose to great wealth. They put on no airs, but thought quite rightly that something was expected of them, so they built a very grand house, furnished it regardless of expense, and when all was finished sent out invitations to an evening party. The cards had R.S.V.P. in one corner, something quite new in our corner of the world. I remember Maggie Lownie, an outspoken spinster, when she met Mrs. Langton in the town, greeted her with :

" ' I've got your card and I'm coming to your party, but what are your hieroglyphics ? '

"Dear me, I remember that party as if it were yesterday. The napkins like everything else were brand new, and old Grandmother Langton, resplendent in black satin and a lace shawl, said, as her napkin skidded for the third time to the floor :

" ' I've surely an awful slippy lap.'

"She was a dear soul and as unpretentious as a daisy. As she looked round at the company and the marvellous supper, she said :

" ' There's nothing my son John likes so much as a bit of toasted cheese to his tea.' "

The school I attended was a small private school, kept by two French ladies. Nothing could have been a greater contrast to my former school, that hive of industry, known as Hutcheson Girls'. Here there was no striving, no competition : it seemed to me a veritable land of afternoons.

I was gratified to find that instead of being the dunce at the bottom of the class I was regarded as advanced in learning to an almost indecent degree. The girls of my age were doing simple sums in multiplication and division : fractions were still beyond their ken, and as for algebra, like Miss Phoebe in *Quality Street*, they did not consider it a ladylike subject. On the other hand, my French had a Britannia-metal quality that was much deplored, and my German was hardly there at all. (No fairy came to my christening to endow me with the gift of tongues.) The English Literature class was taken by a dapper little gentleman, very keen on his work and thankful when he could raise even a spark of interest in his pupils. Thrilled by the way he taught us, for the first time I shone in a class, and at the end of the year carried proudly home a handsome volume, the one and only prize of my life.

There were only about thirty pupils in the school, carefully brought up girls, with well-brushed hair and nice manners. I liked them all and sometimes went to parties at their houses, but I was never intimate with any of them. Brought up with boys, I found girls of my own age difficult to understand. And there was not much time to get to know anyone, our school-day was so ridiculously (though pleasantly) short : from nine-thirty till two, with a break at noon, when we devoured scones and drank milk. I used sometimes to wonder what I was doing in this placid backwater of education, what had made my parents choose such a school? It pleased me very well, but it certainly did not fit one for the battle of life.

Hitherto I had only known Edinburgh as a place to pass through on our way from Fife to Tweeddale, and it was thrilling to live in Pet Marjorie's Conspicuous Town.

John had given me the previous Christmas Dr. John Brown's book containing his account of this amazing child. I was enthralled by the picture he drew of Sir Walter Scott going for her in the snowstorm—" onding o' snaw," and carrying her back in the neuk of his plaid to his house in Castle Street and there playing with her for hours. He would read ballads to her, and she would repeat to him Constance's speeches in *King John* like one possessed. Everything about the child was so lovable, " her vivacity, her passion for nature, for swine, for all living things, her reading, her satire, her frankness, her little sins and rages, her great repentances." She was a good hater, and we were entirely at one with her in her poem about Mary Queen of Scots :

> " Queen Mary was much loved by all,
> Both by the great and by the small.
> But hark ! her soul to heaven doth rise !
> And I suppose she has gained a prize.
> But there is one thing I must tell,
> Elizabeth went to fire and hell ;
> He who would teach her to be civil
> It must be her great friend the divil."

and we went about repeating, until we were ordered to desist, the sad fate of ' three turkeys fair ' :

> " The rats their very bones have crunched,
> Into eternity they're launched,
> A direful death indeed they had
> As wad put any parent mad :
> But she was more than usual calm,
> She did not give a single dam."

My music teacher lived in Queen Street, so it was easy for me to visit Castle Street on my way home and stand and stare at No. 39.

Royal Terrace was another place that had a fascination for me. The Walkers had a friend whose house was in that high-set place, by name Watty Dundas, but always to me The White Knight. He had the same high forehead and gentle surprised eyes as Alice's friend, and the same passion for repeating poems, long but very beautiful. He was very learned, I had been told, an authority on all sorts of things, but he wore his learning lightly. Sometimes he asked me to tea on a Saturday afternoon, and that was a great treat. Apart from the excellent tea provided by his old house-keeper, there were treasures in the way of picture-books which I was allowed to handle at my pleasure, and—best of all—I found that in the early dark of a winter evening I could see from this ' quarter deck of Edinburgh ' my old friend the Inchkeith Light.

Another house I sometimes visited on a Saturday after-noon was that of a grand-aunt, the eldest sister of my father's mother. It was a perfect specimen of an Early-Victorian interior. Nothing had been changed, I suppose, since about 1850. It was ugly, but there was something attractive in its very ugliness, for the materials and work-manship had been of the very best, and each bit of furni-ture had been ' kept ' meticulously through the years.

There were two daughters whom I was told to call Cousin Annie and Cousin Janet. They looked very much alike, with hair parted in the middle and brushed smoothly back into neat coils, dresses tightly buttoned down the front with the high collars fastened with large cameo brooches. Their faces were gentle and withdrawn, and they made me so nervous that when I was alone with them I spoke without intermission, telling them everything I knew in the hope of lighting one spark of interest in their eyes. But I never did. " Quiet did quiet remain."

Great-aunt Elliot herself was strangely young compared to her daughters. She was a gay, pretty old lady with a lace cap with lappets on her silver hair, and over a soft grey dress wore a fluffy white shawl. Father once told me that she had been the beauty of the family, and she still had the air of expecting homage. It was obvious that she was her daughters' whole life : they seemed to exist merely to keep the lamp of her life burning.

We got on together admirably, Great-aunt and I, for she was interested in everything. I told her of my brothers, our home, of Violet, and the games we had played : about the Walkers and the people I met there. She even wanted to know the names of the girls at school, and wondered if they were the grandchildren of this one or that with whom she had once danced. It did not seem incongruous to hear her speak of dancing, she could still, one felt sure, make a pretty figure at it. One day, when I was saying good-bye after a happy hour with her, she said as she looked at me buttoned up in an ulster, with a Cossack fur cap on my curls :

" Off you go to fight the east wind. I used to enjoy doing battle with it. Oh, I wish I were young again, as young as you, Anna."

Her tone more than her words startled me. I had thought—when I thought of it at all—that the old accepted their limitations patiently, that they were glad that the long day's task was over and rest in sight. This desire to be young again seemed to me horribly pathetic and a little unseemly. Very earnestly—with some dim idea of comforting her—I reminded my great-aunt that it wasn't much fun to be young, too much was expected of one, and, anyway, it wasn't as if being young was any guarantee of going on living.

Great-aunt was tired.

" Quite true, child," she said. " The young may die, the old must. Run away now. Bethia will be waiting for you."

Here was another of the indignities of being young. Bethia, the old housemaid, was sent with me to see me home. Not that I objected to Bethia, indeed I was very grateful to her.

The teas at Great-aunt's were not suitable for a hungry school-girl. Everything was good, but there was so little of it—tiny hot scones in a silver dish, wafers of bread and butter, queen cakes that melted in the mouth and left one as hungry as ever. One afternoon Bethia put on the table a plate of large, filling, currant buns. Cousin Janet looked at them, and said in her gentle, cold voice :

" Bethia likes a vulgar fullness."

So did I!

But it was galling not to be allowed to go home alone. Bethia, in a circular waterproof and elastic-sided boots, spoiled everything. It was my desire to go along Princes Street and see the tall ' lands ' of the Old Town lit and peering down, but Bethia decided, naturally, on the shortest way. How could one ponder on the glory of Old Edinburgh, and try to picture Prince Charlie as he held all too brief state in Holyroodhouse, when common decency made it necessary to carry on a certain amount of conversation with one's companion—and very uninteresting conversation it was, for Bethia knew her place and made only the briefest replies to my efforts.

Although I was happy in Edinburgh, very much at home with the Walkers and their friends, and actually enjoying school, I longed desperately to be with my own people again, and when in June came the astonishing news that I had got another brother I begged and prayed to be allowed to come home. I could have lessons at home, I pointed out, and later attend lectures at Queen Margaret College, and in the end, like the Importunate Widow, I prevailed by my much asking.

Of course, when the end of the term came, I was a little sad to leave. I had got much kindness from many people, and was honestly attached to the Walkers, to whom I felt I owed a debt. They had done their best to put my feet in the right way, though ' the D.D.' was perhaps rather cruel in his methods.

65   E

Mrs. Walker took me on Sunday to a strange church to hear a noted preacher, and afterwards, at lunch, I remarked that the woman whose pew we sat in had offered us a million Bibles.

" Dear me," said Dr. Walker mildly, and all that week, if there were strangers at a meal, he never failed to say :

" An extraordinary thing happened last Sunday at St. George's. Anna was offered a million Bibles."

I got so sick of this statement that I could have screamed, and was covered with shame and confusion of face.

On Saturday, when the White Knight was at luncheon, I nearly disgraced my years when the story was again repeated, by breaking into loud sobs. If he had become facetious, as so many had done, or looked sorry for me and changed the subject, I would have wept, but he merely looked interested.

" Why, Anna," he said, " you belong to my school of thought. I never came under a million. ' Bet you a million pounds I'll touch that post before you.' Always a million."

How I blessed him !

CHAPTER V

"If ever you have looked on better days,
If ever been where bells have knolled to church."
As You Like It.

IT was strange to have a tiny baby in the house. When
I went home I heard that Marget had announced his
arrival when she went up to waken Willie and Walter
(John was away) with :

" Ye've gotten a little brother this morning."

Between Marget and Willie there was always a sort of
subterranean feud which broke out once in a while, and
this time Willie felt that he had just cause for wrath. He
got up remarking, " Well, *that's* a lie anyway," and pushed
Marget out of the room.

The baby was christened Alastair but he was seldom
called by that name. The first time John saw him he said,
" Hullo ! Peter," and Peter he was for the first few years.
When he began to develop a personality of his own he
was re-named ' the Mhor '—Gaelic for ' the great one.'
Thus was greatness thrust upon him.

He was a plain baby, and grew into a very plain little
boy, with a rather Mongolian cast of countenance. He
had his own name for each of us. John was Dodo, Willie
was Belee, Walter was Ney, and I was Nana. From the
first he belonged specially to me. Mother was busy with
a multitude of things, housekeeping, church work, and a
certain amount of public work. That winter the Member
of Parliament for our division of Glasgow, Mr. Cameron
Corbett (afterwards Lord Rowallan), had offered to finance
cooking-classes where housewives could learn to make
nourishing meals at little cost. This scheme appealed to

my practical mother and she threw herself into it with enthusiasm. The meetings were in the evening and sometimes kept her rather late, and it was always on those late nights that the poor baby wakened and cried himself into a frenzy. The nursemaid was never kept up, and it fell to me to lift Peter and try to placate him. I always began by walking him up and down the room, humming to him soothingly, and sometimes that worked, but often in desperation I took him downstairs and let the boys take a turn of him. He would stiffen himself and yell in a most alarming way, and when mother did come in we shouted reproachfully, " Here's your baby for you, almost in a fit," and she would take the poor little ' begrutten ' fellow into her arms and comfort him, with such a look on her face of utter content that it has remained with me always.

My education was supposed to continue at home, and I did have lessons in French and music and drawing, and later on I went to Queen Margaret College. But the only real education I ever had was listening to Father and the boys talking.

John was at Glasgow University that year, Willie and Walter at school. John's first class was at 8 a.m., and as he liked to walk the four miles across the city it meant leaving the house before seven o'clock. We would hear through our dreams Marget's voice asking him on the dark foggy mornings, " Did ye mind yer cod-liver oil ? " and then the bang of the front door.

Already John had begun to write and had had some essays and short stories accepted by *Macmillan's*, *The Gentleman's Magazine*, and *Blackwood's*. About that time he wrote a short novel, called *Sir Quixote of the Moors*. It is dedicated to Gilbert Murray, who was then Professor of Greek at Glasgow, and is " an episode in the life of the Sieur de

Rohaine." It ends with the hero riding away from the lady he loves, loving honour more.

Evidently the American publishers had not approved of this ending, and in the American edition a final paragraph is added :

" I cannot recall my thoughts during that ride : I seem not to have thought at all. All I know is that in about an hour there came into my mind, as from a voice, the words : ' Recreant ! Fool ! ' and I turned back."

The other day I found a diary kept for a few months when I was about seventeen. It is full of such items as :

> " Read paper to meeting on Hannah More,
> " Collected for Foreign Missions,
> " Recited Barrie at Samaritan Hospital,
> " Went to Band of Hope,"

which seems to show that I led a blameless but an appallingly dull life. I don't think, though, that I found it dull. At home there was the young brother, who became more of an interest every day ; and many small duties and distractions and pleasures. Church work was quite enjoyable. Meeting the people in their own homes one realised how fine they were, hard-working, self-sacrificing, patient —and with such a sense of humour ! Ours was, with a few exceptions, a working-class congregation, and though many of them had a hard struggle to live they enjoyed life in an amazing way.

We thought, my brothers and I, that we were singularly fortunate to be with such human, interesting people, and not in a suburban church where so often gentility reigns. Knox's people found everything in their church, their social as well as their spiritual life. It was the centre of everything to them. Only the other day a man came to see us who had been a youth in Knox's in my father's time, and as he talked about the old days I was surprised to find how much he remembered and brought back to my recollection. When I remarked on it he said :

" Well, those days are the happiest things I've got to think about."

One very likeable thing about Glasgow people is that they never mind laughing at themselves. An undersized, bow-legged little man once remarked :

" My grandfather was a fine big man, six feet three ; he would laugh if he saw me," and he so obviously enjoyed the joke that one had to laugh with him.

To visit their homes, whether on an errand of mercy or collecting for Zenana Missions, was always a pleasure. Their welcome was so sincere, and what they gave they gave so willingly. Now and again one came on a complaining poor soul, who would say in answer to a question about her health, " Oh, just hanging by a tack," and enter into a detailed account of her many ailments, but generally their cheerful courage was something to wonder at.

One woman, who lived in a tenement overlooking a railway line, had a great desire to travel. She used to watch the London Express pass every morning, with its shining dining-car, and say to her daughter, " Aweel, there's ma denner awa' by again."

There was one house where I was made particularly welcome, the abode of the Simpsons. Mr. Simpson had a butcher's shop—which may have accounted for the well-fed look of his large young family—and when a christening took place an immense roast of beef always graced the laden tea-table. It was my privilege to be present at one of those occasions, and my neighbour, a portly man, having mopped up with bread the last of the rich gravy on his plate, turned to me and said in tones of deep conviction. " This is a grand house for flesh."

It was Mrs. Simpson who said of a visiting minister who preached an unconscionable time, " My ! I thought yon man was rowed up for a week."

One seldom came away from a house without having heard something that amused or touched one—and that is more than can be said of most social contacts.

My father, assisted by one or two of the young men, ran a small magazine for the congregation, called ' The Visitor,' which once a month was distributed in the district, in the hope of interesting some of the many who attended no church. When I was sent with copies I poked them through the letter-box, if there happened to be such a thing, being too shy to ring a bell and bring someone to the door. Once I accompanied another young woman and was amazed at the aplomb with which she addressed each householder.

" This is ' The Visitor.' Chilly, isn't it ? "

But I never attained to such heights.

It would be about this time that John acquired a Sunday School class of eight very bad small boys. He delighted in them, and there is no doubt that they were the originals of the Gorbals Die-hards in *Huntingtower*. It is probable that he learned more from them than they learned from him. When he spoke to them on the lesson for the day they were often reminded by it of some experience of their own. They nodded their heads over the story of the sick man let down through the roof, and said they had seen a sailor in merry mood dancing on a bakehouse, and *he* went down through the roof. When the lesson was over John told them a story, which caused great excitement and went on serially from Sunday to Sunday. The hero was a missionary, which was supposed to make it suitable for Sunday School.

Mother, I am sure, was relieved when John's departure

for Oxford made a new teacher necessary. She could not believe that this tale of an adventurous missionary was what the children needed, but John parted with regret from his tough little scholars, and chose with care a gift for each of them.

The children of the Gorbals were amusing small people, a mixture of gaiety, impudence, and misery. When Mother asked some boys playing ' bools ' on the street if they went to any Sunday School, one snub-nosed little fellow leered up at her and said :

" Ach, we're what ye ca' Jews."

The Band of Hope was where I became acquainted with them ; they turned up there in force every Friday night through the winter. One evening I remember very distinctly. The hall was packed with children, many of them with bare feet, and the atmosphere on entering made one recoil. The President was away ill, and the decent little man who took his place had no idea how to keep order. He began well with :

" Now, boys and girls, do you want to grow up drunkards ? "

There was a unanimous shout of " No."

The second attempt was not so successful.

" Boys and girls, do you want to grow up topers ? "

The second yell was quite as unanimous : " Yes."

At this the poor man was rather nonplussed, but he continued. " You mean you want to be abstainers ? That's right. Never touch anything stronger than milk. I'll tell you a story about a Bedouin who fed his wife on milk till she got that fat she could hardly walk."

The children received this with shouts of laughter, and the absurdity of the story seemed also to strike the speaker, and he went on : " Of course it's all right to be kind to your wife, but to feed her on milk till she canna walk is fair ridiculous."

His audience, seeing no immediate end to this tale, rapidly grew restive, and it was announced there would be a song.

No censorship seemed to exist on what sort of song might be sung, and a small damsel mounted the platform and sang a ribald ditty about a certain young woman who had lost her lover at the Fair, but expected confidently to acquire another " gin Ne'er-day."

After that pandemonium reigned, and I was trying to separate two boys who were beating each other on the head when the door opened and Father came in.

What a yell of welcome from the children ! And when he began to speak, what a blessed calm.

Often I had wondered how Father with his passion for Nature and all country sights and sounds could bear to spend his life among grimy city streets with such cheerfulness and seeming content, and that night I learned his secret. It was not merely a crowd of little dirty children he was looking at, he saw them as the young generation that might help to make all things new. A Band of Hope ! There was simply no end to what he hoped for those children and for the City of Glasgow. He could have cried with the poet :

> " *Show me the town they saw*
> *Withouten fleck or flaw* . . ."

It is a misfortune for a minister's daughter to be entirely without music. Although I had had music lessons practically all my life I was no use at playing accompaniments and I couldn't sing a note. At social meetings specially, I felt my shortcomings sadly.

One night I got an idea. A course of lectures was

organised every winter in our part of Glasgow, and well-known people came from London and elsewhere and spoke on their own special subject. On the night of which I write a dramatic recital was the bill of fare—to my delight, as I had a passion for the drama. A well-known actor and actress gave some scenes from Shakespeare, as well as various sketches and readings. As I listened entranced, the thought came to me, " Why shouldn't I do that? " I had inherited, in some degree, my father's speaking voice and his good memory, and I had a small gift as a mimic. At first I only attempted what I had seen done, but as I gained experience and a certain amount of self-confidence, I chose things to suit my audience. J. M. Barrie was a mine of wealth. Having lived as a child on the East Coast, the Kirriemuir tongue was easy to me, and the church people never grew tired of Barrie's humour. One hardly realises how good those portraits of village folk are until one sees one's audience rock with laughter at the truth of them. Sometimes it must be admitted, they are over-drawn, the pawkiness (horrible word) especially, and the pathos is apt to degenerate into " the mild saut tear beloved in Zion." But the conversation at the Pigsty Club, Waster-Luny's feverish search for Ezra when he thought the minister was waiting till he found it, and his remarks on ancestors, " Is it no' a queer thing that you and me has nae ancestors? They're as lost to sicht as a flagon lid fallen ahint the dresser," delighted me as much as my audience. J. J. Bell's classic *Wee Macgreegor* was another sure winner. I enjoyed letting myself go in the speech of the Gorbals. My enjoyment was, however, not shared by two genteel ladies at a concert, who were overheard saying :

" What can her mother be thinking about to let her speak that vulgar broad Scotch ; and quite a refined-looking girl too."

About the time John went to Oxford he became a 'reader' to John Lane at the Bodley Head, who published his novel *John Burnet of Barns*, and also *Grey Weather* and *A Lost Lady of Old Years*.

John Burnet of Barns is a story of Tweeddale in the seventeenth century. He began to write it when he was about sixteen, and into it he put all his passion for that delectable land. Reading it lately after many years I thought how good it was, mannered a little, perhaps, but so young and ardent and alive. He knew the hills and glens that he wrote about like the face of a friend, and it is an endless pleasure to lovers of Tweeddale merely to read the familiar place-names—Dawyck, Stobo, Drummelzier, Stanhope, Powsail Burn, Hopecarton, the Logan Water, the hills of Cardon, Broadlaw, Cademuir.

The book was a great favourite with all of us, even Mhor knew some of John Burnet's adventures. Once, when he was reproved for telling a lie (he said he had found an elephant's nest in the garden) he asked, " And what is *John Burnet* but a lie ? "

Mhor and his antics were a great amusement to his family. All children tell stories into themselves, but the odd thing about Mhor was that he told his openly. He would walk up and down the room, talking to himself, his eyes flashing, his hands gesticulating wildly, entirely oblivious of spectators. Strangers were amazed at the sight, and one visitor asked sadly :

" Is he not quite right ? "

He had a great friend, known only to himself, whom he called Mr. Bathboth of Bathboth. Strange were the ways of this gentleman, as reported by Mhor. And his house. " It's a lovely house," we were told, " it's a public-house."

He was not a precocious child, indeed he was rather behind in his lessons, but when he was five he knew the

Midsummer Night's Dream almost by heart, and long before he could read he was able to repeat the *Jungle Book* stories word by word. He could not bear sad things. ("Does anybody die?" was his first question about a book), but Tennyson's *Morte d'Arthur* so appealed to him that he could not resist having it read to him sometimes as his bed-time poem. It was a funny sight to see him sitting up in bed weeping unwilling tears, and howling with rage at Tennyson for writing such sad, lovely poetry and at himself for listening to it.

As a child he never approved of the Sabbath. "I'm as dull as a bull and as sick as a daisy," he would tell us as church-time approached. He didn't like angels, and he wanted to be a jockey. He was apt to pick up expressions from his brothers and their friends.

One day he was displeased with every member of his family, and looking round the table with a bitter smile, he said:

"I was playing quite quietly in Heaven when God came and said to me, 'Mhor, you've to go and live with the Buchans.' I said, 'The *Buchans*? Good *Lord*.'"

In spite of his horror at the thought of being a Buchan he must have found us not so bad, for one night he woke up in his little bed beside me, and sitting up and staring wildly round, he said:

"Well, it's a good thing *that's* not true anyway."

He told me the dream. It seemed that he was on a beautiful golden ship with silver sails, sailing away to Heaven, when he met another ship, a horrible black one, bound for quite a different destination, and to his dismay he recognised among the passengers on board *all the members of his family.*

"And what did you do, Mhor?" I asked, and the poor child gave a great gulp and said angrily:

76

"I came on beside you."

John went to Brasenose College with a scholarship, and at first, I think, he must have been rather anxious about ways and means. In a letter to Willie, written in his first term, he says :

"My college bills for the week come only to 17s. You see I have been so much out at meals. I find that at the end of term we have certain payments to make : this has completely stumped me ! . . . A good many copies of my book have been sold, and C. H. D. writes that he has made enquiries at the Glasgow booksellers and finds that it is selling well there. I am prospering pretty well with the *Stanhope*, but it means working in the Bodleian two hours each day, as I have to read all sorts of obscure old books. I have done about two chapters of *John Burnet* since you sent it up. I am being continually pestered by men coming round wanting me to play football. They seem to think that all Scotsmen are heaven-born geniuses at that game. When you come up you will be in great request.

"I am going a long walk this afternoon and then I shall write an article for the *Glasgow Herald*. I must make money.

"Love to the Bird, and Peter and Anna and Father and Mother,

"Your affectionate brother,

"JOHN BUCHAN."

John won the Stanhope Prize, and later on the Newdigate with a poem on the Pilgrim Fathers.

He must have worked with beaver-like industry, but work was no trouble to him, and he also played with zest. Very soon his writing was bringing in a good income, so he had money to do things and could make the most of his time at Oxford.

It was when he was President of the Union that he

suggested that Mother and I should pay a visit to Oxford. It was a thing that he and I had often talked about, but I had never for a moment believed that it would ever come to pass. Oxford in my mind was a fabled city, a many-towered Camelot, something one dreamed of but never reached, and when Mother, after much anxious thought, sighed deeply and said, " Surely nothing can go very far wrong at home in a week, and I might regret it if we didn't go," I was positively bemused with bliss.

It was arranged we should leave on February 9th, and preparations began and new clothes were got, but even when our cases were packed I dared not believe we were really going. Something would happen to prevent us, if not an angel with a flaming sword, at least Mhor would take whooping-cough, or Marget would suddenly feel too old for work and retire (as she sometimes threatened), in which case the whole fabric of our home life would crumble.

On the morning of our departure it seemed too good to be true when everyone came down well and hearty for breakfast, and Marget appeared, positively urbane, to ask if we wanted sandwiches, only to be told we would lunch on the train. A fleeting regret that my old friend of the tenement was not having the chance of her ' denner ' on the train passed through my mind as I supped my porridge, and I hated leaving the Mhor, but nothing really mattered except the stupendous fact that I, too, was to see Oxford.

The journey itself was one long thrill, for it was my first excursion into England. I stared at the little villages grouped round a church and an ivory-covered rectory, and thought they had come straight out of Charlotte M. Yonge. My book lay unread as I sat and dreamed. When John met us I realised by his rather fixed grin that he felt he had let himself in for a big thing, though it was not till later I discovered that a man who has his people up is an object of pity to his friends, who stand chivalrously round to help him through.

He had taken rooms at the Mitre, which in these days was exactly my idea of what an English inn ought to be. One could imagine the stage-coach stopping there, and passengers, cold and hungry, being thawed before blazing fires and given the best of food and drink. Cloaked horsemen probably galloped up at midnight, and perhaps Shakespeare himself stayed in just such a hostelry on his way from London to Stratford.

It was delightful to come down in the morning to the bow-windowed coffee-room and look out at the life of Oxford going past, bakers' boys with crusty loaves, undergraduates in funny little cloaks, neat shop-girls, housewives with basket, and then turn to a table by the fire and such an excellent breakfast.

John spared neither himself nor us in his efforts to entertain. We were dragged at high speed round colleges, up innumerable steps, down to the river, back to luncheon in one college, on to tea in another, varied by a drive out to Blenheim Park with a long walk round the lake. It was all very enjoyable, though slightly disillusioning. Oxford, I found, was not all spires and bells, gray walls and green lawns, there were also endless arid roads of villas. Nor were the undergraduates ' gods of old story ' but very ordinary young men, cheerful and easy to get on with. The Olympians, whom we heard debate in the Union and met at dinner in J. B.'s rooms in the High, were a different matter. I was speechless before them. Mother, on the other hand, was by no means impressed; indeed, when John told her solemnly that these men were probably the Prime Ministers of the future, she was moved to laughter, and merely said :

" Oh, poor things ! They've a long way to go before they're fit to be Prime Ministers."

The last day of our stay I remember as pure pleasure. J. B. had something special to do, so Mother and I spent the morning among the shops, buying small presents to take home. There was a particularly pleasant luncheon-party, and after tea I went out alone and just wandered, gazing at will into antique shops, and fingering books for as long as I pleased. In St. John's Gardens aconites were out—spring, though it came so slowly up our way, would soon be here. There had been a shower and the roofs were glistening in the clear shining after rain ; above Magdalen Tower was a primrose strip of sky, somewhere church bells were ringing. . . .

The high light of the visit to me was going to the theatre that evening to see *Midsummer Night's Dream* done by the O.U.D.S. It was my very first visit to the theatre and I have never forgotten it. I knew the play by heart and now I was to see it in flesh and blood. When the curtain went up on the Palace of Theseus, like Bottom I was 'translated.' I lived with the players : I *was* a player. It was I who as Titania refused Oberon the little changeling boy, who said as Hermia :

"How low am I, thou painted maypole ? speak,"

and replied as Helena :

"She was a vixen, when she went to school " ;

and when at the end Puck said :

"Think but this, and all is mended,
That you have but slumber'd here,"

it was I who wakened from a lovely dream to a workaday world.

The next day we said a grateful farewell to Oxford and a relieved J. B., and went on to London to spend a few days with a relative of Father's known to us as ' Great-uncle-John-in-London.' He and his wife (whom we had been taught to call Aunt John) had settled so comfortably into English ways that they had no intention of ever revisiting their native land. When we were told this, I was honestly horrified. That any Scot would *choose* to die and be buried in England appalled me. Like the dying Borderer I could have said :

> " I've been happy above ground,
> I could ne'er be happy under
> Out of Teviot's gentle sound ;
> Part us then not far asunder."

It almost seemed as if Great-uncle John had a contempt for his native land. When the salad was handed round he would say :

" Salad's a thing you see far too little of in Scotland. Here we know how to appreciate the fruits of the earth."

Mother had warned me never to contradict Uncle John as his heart was weak, but my patience was sorely tried.

He wanted to know what had set John on to writing, and said :

" I never liked scribblers. That R. L. S. that they made so much fuss about—bless my soul, that was a fellow I never could stand. Wore a black shirt. He couldn't write."

It was only the fear of seeing my aged uncle stark on the carpet that kept me from contradicting him dead.

But though he did not approve of R. L. S. he adored Sir Walter, and knew almost as many ballads and old tales as my father did.

Aunt John was something of a character. Younger by many years than her husband, she was a tall handsome woman with a dominating Roman nose. She always dressed richly and had great dignity of manner, so that when she became arch with her husband it was acutely embarrassing. One day she sailed in with a new hat and said :

" Jackie dear, how do you like my *chapeau* ? "

Jackie dear ! How did she dare ?

A notable housekeeper, Aunt John had perfect servants, and everything went like clockwork. Always after dinner, when we were so replete as to be more or less comatose, she read aloud. Her reading gave me great pleasure, especially when she chose one of Ian Maclaren's most pathetic stories, where every sob and every broken utterance was represented by a dash. She rendered it literally with curious effect :

" I dash have come home dash . . ."

I did not dare catch Mother's eye.

This household of elderly people was kept going by Aunt John's niece, Maud Mark, who had been brought up by her aunt. She and I became fast friends at once, and the passing years have strengthened our friendship. Though meeting only occasionally we have never failed to write to each other every week from whatever part of the globe we happened to be in.

This was my first visit to Uncle John and his wife, but it was by no means my last. Aunt John, for whom we all had a great affection, died quite young, but Uncle lived for nearly twenty years beyond the Psalmist's limit, and we had time to deeply appreciate his good heart and endless kindness.

CHAPTER VI

" We were young,
We were merry,
We were very very wise "

MARY COLERIDGE.

LOOKING back from an age when the years fly faster than leaves in an autumn gale, it seems to me that in my youth time ' stood still withal ' and large tracts of un-occupied time lay all about one.   How else could one have had time to read Dumas, Hardy, Meredith, George Eliot, the Brontës, Jane Austen, Thackeray, not to speak of the poets ?

The end of the 'nineties was an exciting time for a girl to grow up and become acquainted with writers.   There was the Yellow Book circle gathered round ' Mr. Lane of Vigo St.,' who was accused of discovering a new poet every morning, as well as a whole host of young authors.

Poets to me seemed marvellous, almost fabulous crea-tures.   I quite believed that if you tracked one to his home you found :

" . . . he ate his supper in a room
    Blazing with lights, four Titians on the wall,
And twenty naked girls to change his plate."

The first poet I ever saw did look like that.   Richard Le Gallienne was in Glasgow lecturing and he came to see John about something.   He was tall and slim with hyacinthine locks and a flowing tie, a beautiful voice and captivating manners.

Father and I went to hear him lecture.   What his sub-ject was I have no recollection ; I only remember that he told us he had been shaved by a lady barber, and when she said :

83

" Aren't you afraid I cut you ? " he had replied :

" Ah, no, ladies *never* cut me."

(" Impudent fellow," said Father, in a disgusted aside.)

We were fortunate to have among our friends all kinds and conditions. People who are only intimate with their own set must have a very dull time ; though, it is to be confessed, I suffered as a child from our parents' desire to make us good mixers. (When a party was on the carpet Father had what seemed to me a really horrid way of asking all and sundry. He would come in full of a lame boy who had never been to a party and whom he had invited. Being an arrant little snob, I complained that I could never have a pretty party ; it was always spoiled by some shabbily dressed guests to whom we were expected to devote more time and attention than to our own friends, and I used to wonder what sort of party resulted from the ' highways and hedges ' invitation.)

We had the church people, to whom we were deeply attached, and all the kind hospitable Glasgow people who lived round us. There were, too, the University professors and their wives, and life was greatly enriched for me when we got to know many of the Glasgow artists.

Certainly the parties we attended were varied, ranging from a christening party at the butcher's where ' flesh ' was a feature of the entertainment, to an ' evening ' at an opulent villa, where everything was of the best, including the manners of the considerate host, who, when cards were suggested and he feared as a minister's daughter I might not want to play, said, " All right, you play cards and Anna and I'll play a wee house " ; or a sedate professorial dinner-party.

To me as a young girl dinner-parties were a penance. I was shy and exceedingly diffident of my power to converse with anyone of intelligence. Only now and again did I meet someone who made me feel happy and at ease. Such a one was Walter Raleigh, then Professor of English Literature in Glasgow. The first time I met him I was almost sick with fright, but he began by confiding in me that when he wore a tie in a knot he looked so cadaverous that everyone insisted he was overworking, but if he wore a bunchy bow-tie he was almost invariably congratulated on his healthy appearance. Then he confessed that he loathed a dress kilt, and thought a man sitting in a chintz-covered chair in a kilt was a disgusting sight. From that, somehow or other, we got on to Shakespeare and I was on the top of the world, everything forgotten except the interest of the talk.

Perhaps the most enjoyable parties we attended were at the Camerons' house. Everyone knows D. Y. Cameron's pictures, and the exquisite water-colours of his sister Katharine, but all the members of that large family were gifted. Katharine was one of the youngest, and already distinguished when we met and became friends. She was —and, happily, is—a beloved person. Her large brown eyes seemed full of Celtic melancholy, but she was really the gayest of creatures, and had moments of being wildly funny. Her studio was enchanted ground to me and I was proud to sit to her as a model when she wanted one. Believing all things and hoping all things, she was an incorrigible optimist. Once when I was staying with her in the country she rushed into my room at 4 a.m. on May-day, shouting :

"Get up, Nan, and let's go out and wash our faces in May dew and we'll be beautiful all the year."

That the charm did not work depressed her not at all.

Katharine had a charming taste in dress, her clothes were never 'arty' but always just a little different from other people's clothes, and just right for herself. She did much for me in the way of improving my appearance, helping me to choose becoming clothes and making me stop torturing my hair with dozens of hairpins. I still possess a photograph of myself in a picture-hat of her composition. The Mhor rather oddly is also in the picture. After seeing artists' rooms it was not surprising that our Mid-Victorian drawing-room should seem to me quite unendurable. It was a pleasant home-like room hardly altered, as far as furniture went, from the room Mother came to as a bride. The rosewood furniture was the same, the chiffonier with the marble top, the red rep curtains and chair covers, the large gilt mirrors. The walls were covered with a perfect network of cords from which hung faded flower studies, enlarged photographs, and plush-framed plaques. A presentation clock in alabaster, supported by gilt cupids, stood on a bracket. At first, Mother was indignant at the idea of changing anything, but being a very understanding person she remembered from her own youth how girls felt about things, remembered also how her own mother said, " Never daunton youth," and let me have my will.

In her heart, I think, she was rather proud of having an ' artistic ' drawing-room. It was many years later when she and I were talking in our house at Peebles, that she said suddenly and vindictively :

" I can hardly forgive you when I think how you put away the things your father showed me so proudly when we got home to the manse in Perth on our wedding-day."

And by that time the years had taught me much, and I knew just what she felt.

The room when finished pleased me greatly. It had a plain cream paper, a blue self-coloured carpet, and blue curtains : the chairs and sofa had loose covers of printed linen, old china that had lived a safe and secluded life in a cupboard was brought out to shine bravely in blue and

rose and gold. A Georgian mirror from Broughton Green
that had languished in a bedroom because its gilt was rather
tarnished got a place of honour over the fireplace. A few
Medici prints of famous pictures, given me from time to
time by John, hung on the walls, and low bookcases held
my most precious books, which also came from the same
source : Thackeray, Jane Austen, Dorothy Osborne's
Letters, Kenneth Grahame's *Pagan Papers* and *The Golden
Age*, Kipling, Stevenson, Sir Walter Scott's *Diary*, *Peter
Ibbetson* and *Trilby*, an edition of Shakespeare, two stout
volumes of Browning, Keats, Shelley ; *The Oxford Book
of English Verse* ; meek little volumes like *Goody Two-shoes*,
A Flat-Iron for a Farthing, and a very early edition of Hans
Andersen's *The Will o' the Wisps are in Town*, and many
others.

So far so good, but I did not stop there. With some
idea of being Yellow Bookish I kept the blinds well down,
and burned sticks of incense. I had a great desire to look
like an Aubrey Beardsley heroine, with a curly mouth and
slanting eyes, but that being physically impossible I had
to content myself with sitting in a darkened room smelling
of incense.

My family bore it patiently for a little, but one afternoon
Father came in, fell over a footstool and into one of his
infrequent rages. Pulling the blinds up to the top he
shouted :

" Why should we sit in darkness and a horrible stink ? "
Then turning to me, lolling on the sofa among cushions, he
said : " Get up, girl, and don't sit attitudinising there."

One can get very much up against people by changing
rooms. Children, especially, loathe change. John's children always spent the summer with us in a little house in
Broughton belonging to my mother. (It rejoiced in the
festive-sounding name of Gala Lodge, but the name had

a grim significance. It stood on the Gala Hill— corruption of Gallows Hill—where once rough justice was meted out.) The house had been practically untouched for nearly a century, and one spring we had the whole place papered and painted and partly refurnished—throwing away cartloads of rubbish. We were very pleased with the result, but when the children came their wrath knew no bounds. They rushed like mad things through the house, filling the air with their lamentations.

"*Where's* the stuffed pheasant with the medal round its neck?"

"Oh, you couldn't have been so *wicked* as to put away The Deacons' Trip!"

"You didn't burn Nicodemus?"

And then in heartbroken accents: "Didn't you know Gala Lodge was our idea of Heaven?"

We made one change in our Glasgow house that winter which was a complete success. Mother decided that as Mhor spent all his time with his family I might have the nursery to make into a study for the boys, leaving Father in peace in his own study. It was a sunny room looking out on the garden, easy to make pleasant with pale yellow walls and paint. A joiner made two shelves for books to stand on the ugly mantelpiece. A many-coloured Indian rug covered the old cork carpet, the much-kicked and hacked nursery table was stained, and made a strong and roomy writing-table. Father presented a comfortable armchair, and the old nursery chairs had new cushions on their hard seats. It was meant to be a surprise for J. B. when he came home from Oxford in December, and he was delighted with it. At once he stacked all the books he was studying at the moment on the writing-table, along with the MSS. he was reading for John Lane, put out some College groups, and the room was complete.

MYSELF WHEN YOUNG, WITH ALASTAIR.

Many happy hours I spent curled in the arm-chair with a book while John worked. I knew better than to interrupt, but every now and again he would get up and stand on the fender with his back to the fire and talk, and then I was ready, like an affectionate terrier, to be all attention and fall in with any mood.

Often, of course, there were people with John in his study, and I had to absent myself from felicity for a while. Our house was generally littered with friends of my brothers, and always one or two spent the summer holidays with us wherever we happened to be, and, as a rule, a girl friend of my own, and if we were far out of the way of shops Mother must have found the catering far from easy. One friend of John's arrived to stay, a fishing-basket holding all he deemed necessary for a fortnight's visit. On the Sunday Mother, always a frank and fearless commentator, said something must be done to make Richard look respectable for church, but the only improvement she could think of was a pair of gloves. Richard had a soul above mundane matters, and he accepted the gloves obediently, and stalked along looking rather like a heron with his long thin legs in very tight knickerbockers, quite heedless of our ill-bred sniggers as we walked behind.

There was always much talk and laughter in our house. A visitor, accused by Mother of sitting silent, replied:

" Silent! It's as much as one can do to listen in this house," and we did not gather from her tone that she got any pleasure from what she heard.

Books were our favourite topic. What was said of Maria Edgeworth's house was true of ours—" literature is not a treat for company on invitation days, but is actually the daily bread of the family."

There was no constraint between parents and children. When I was arguing with Father one day about the doctrines of Freewill and Foreordination he got very bored with me and remarked as he rose from the table :

" I sometimes think you are a very ignorant creature." I was too !

Though we liked to pretend that we had got far beyond all old-fashioned beliefs, we knew in our hearts that they were what we would always hold on to—the foundation of our lives. Our parents gave us the richest gift young people can have, the feeling of being loved and treasured beyond words, and they made it plain to us that they cared far more that we should be good—just simple, happy good —than that we should attain to riches and honour.

Mother often deplored that she cared so much for public opinion. It was a grief to her that Father, who cared nothing at all about what people thought and said of him, seemed always to be on the unpopular side. At Assembly time, when all the dignitaries of the Church, as well as the rank and file, were gathered in Edinburgh in May, it was bitter to her to sit in the Moderator's Gallery and hear Father make a speech that met with disfavour from the majority. On one occasion a stranger said to her :

" Who is that disagreeable minister ? " and Mother replied coldly :

" He comes from Glasgow."

It was odd that Father in public should be such a fighter, for if ever a man carried in his right hand gentle peace it was he. In every small way he gave in to Mother, but if it were a question of what he believed to be right he was adamant.

One spring, after a heavy winter's work in the church, Mother collapsed, and for a short time was acutely ill. John had to be sent for, and we were aghast at the pit that had opened so suddenly before our unsuspecting feet. What made it worse was that Marget was called away to nurse a sick relative, and we had only a young girl in the kitchen. One often hears about the trouble nurses make in a house, but I shall always bless the nurse who saw us through that time. I was miserably conscious of my short-comings as a housekeeper as I stood, with a cookery book in one hand, trying to make a pudding for the evening meal, or grilling chops till they had neither taste nor nourishment left in them. Nurse Strang pretended to enjoy her meals, but I fear it was out of pity for my flushed face and anxious eyes.

It was quite a long time before Mother got back her strength, and though I did my best to take her place I was a wretched substitute. There was a terrible monotony about the food I provided, and sausages appeared so often (without the excuse of a war) that John asked if I had been left a bequest of sausages, and Willie said I had discovered a sausage mine.

But we got over that bad patch: Mother was well, Marget came back, and the house was its comfortable self again.

In the June following, John took me to climb in Switzer-land. We had climbed many of the Scottish hills, including the Skye Coolins, but now we entered into the treasures of the snow.

It was new to J. B., as it was to me, and what a grand time we had!

Zermatt, that famous haunt of climbers, was our base. The evening we arrived we went out after dinner, walked along the winding road that leads to the Schwarzsee and gazed at the mighty peak of the Matterhorn, while John told me of Whymper's first ascent. It was hardly the moment, I felt, to visit the graves of the first victims, of Croz, the guide, of Hudson and the boy Hadow. The text on one stone caught my eye—*Be ye therefore also ready.*

It was too much. I went back to the hotel feeling I was doomed, and was in no way cheered by John's conversation about climbers' boots coming off as they whirled down from the heights.

However, June is too early for serious climbing, and there was no great danger in what we attempted. I can still feel the freshness of those mornings when we set on at 3 a.m. with Joseph and Aloys, the guides, tramping in single file through meadows full of wild flowers drenched with dew, into a wood where we got glimpses of snow peaks through tall straight pines, up and up till we reached the snow. As we returned, stumbling down with the skin rubbed off our toes, puffs of hot scented air came up to meet us, the tinkle of cowbells greeted us, and as we threw ourselves down on the seat outside the hotel our favourite waiting maid would enquire solicitously :

" Thé complet, m'sieur ? " and John would reply :

" Thé *très* complet," by which he meant not only rolls and butter, but honey and mixed biscuits as well.

The next summer we went to Chamonix, and climbed most of the Aiguilles, nearly meeting our end on an ice slope. That, too, was a perfect holiday. It was not only the climbing that made it such fun, it was the pleasure we took in each other's company. We found a copy of *The Brass Bottle* and read it together, laughing till we were quite helpless ; and how we talked ! Something would start us off and we would go on for hours, capping each other's quotations, recalling lovely things in books, planning what we would do in the years to come.

It was the next year, in the summer of 1901, when John was at the Bar, and sub-editor of the *Spectator*, that he was asked to go to South Africa as one of Lord Milner's secretaries.

We were on holiday in Peeblesshire when he wired the news to us, and said he was coming up to talk over things. I met him at Broughton station with the pony-trap, and the pony, a volatile animal, bolted as we got on to the high road.

" Cautious, Nan," John said, with mock solemnity " remember you carry Cæsar and all his fortunes."

We had only about ten days to get used to the thought of his going, and he was gone. What made it doubly hard for Mother was that her indomitable old mother was lying hopelessly ill, and she grudged every minute away from her, while longing to be with her boy.

John sailed in September, two days before our grandmother died. Then, as sometimes happens, events followed quickly. Father was asked to go to South Africa to take someone's place for nine months. At first it was thought that the difficulties in the way were insurmountable, but somehow they were overcome, and it was decided that he and Mother and the Mhor would sail in December. Willie was at Oxford, Walter at Glasgow University, I was to roam at large.

The house was advertised to let, and among the people who came to look at it were members of a sect who called themselves ' Bible Christians.' We never discovered what they believed, or did not believe, but they seemed harmless creatures, and Father was in favour of letting them have the house at a very low rent. They hailed from America and seemed rather confused by the ways of this country.

The coal-cellar was full, also the jam-cupboard, and Mother asked if they would care to take over the contents. They said they would have to ask the Lord, and came back later to tell us that they might take the coal but not the jam, which made Mother so sorry for them that she promptly bestowed on them the jam.

Mother naturally felt that to cross the ocean was a tremendous undertaking, and she could not believe that we would ever again be reunited as a family, or that things would ever be the same. It does make one realise what a comparatively gentle thing war was then, when people could actually take a trip to a country at war.

There were so many farewells to be said that everyone was rather thankful when the day of departure arrived. The Mhor bore himself with dignity until he found himself in the train for Southampton, when he flung himself on the floor, shouting :

" I don't want to leave my native land."

The trip was on the whole a great success, in spite of the fact that Father got a touch of the sun, Mother was poisoned by a mosquito-sting and the Mhor nearly perished through a surfeit of tinned milk. Mother wrote most amusing letters, full of descriptions of the people she met and the strange things she saw. Port Elizabeth was their headquarters and she was shocked at the war prices there, a shilling for a cauliflower ! In our war we would think ourselves lucky to pay so little.

Father was no letter-writer (we used to say that he would walk miles to deliver a message rather than write one) in spite of the fact that he published a slender volume of poems, a book of essays, and wrote a long romance about the Covenanters, which appeared serially in a religious weekly. His letters consisted of bleak sentences, such as :

" What a beautiful blue the ocean is ! " " The veldt is very much what I expected," and gave us little or no information.

The Mhor wrote oily little notes in pencil (his hands being anointed for mosquito-bites), which invariably ended, " Now I must finch up."

We at home were meantime leading a blameless life.

I paid a number of visits and nearly had a nervous breakdown through being consistently pleasant for so long. It was a blessed relief to go to Peebles and be with my own people.

The old house on the bridge had given us all a liking for living in a street. Lying in bed in the morning we could hear what kind of day it was from passers-by.

" Grand mornin', Tam."

" Ay, but a nippin' wind."

We could even hear the news of the town as the people, passing to their work, stopped to chat, and it gave one a cosy feeling of rubbing shoulders with one's kind.

The Peebles house had an odd but pleasant smell which we attributed to the parrot, which inhabited a large cage in the hall, but after the parrot had passed away the intriguing smell still continued, so we decided it was the odour not of sanctity but of good living. In that house only the best butter was used for cooking, and lashings of cream. Sweetmeats there were in abundance, opulent chocolates and boxes of Edinburgh rock. In these days of margarine and national bread, spam and dried eggs, it is almost painful to remember the breakfasts—' rizzered haddies,' kidneys and bacon, poached eggs and fried tomatoes on toast, new-made baps, farm butter and home-made marmalade.

Two aunts and an uncle lived in this house, which adjoined the Bank in which our grandfather had carried on his business as a banker and lawyer and was succeeded by his son. Writer is the Scots word for lawyer, and our grandfather's plate is still on the red door, announcing with truth, after a century, that Mr. Buchan, Writer, lives within. (A small boy invited to drink tea with his favourite author, gazing at the plate, said, " Would it not be better to put ' Mr. Buchan, Author ' ? ")

Aunt Kate, the younger aunt, was pretty, as I remember her, with hazel eyes, coal-black hair, and a bright colour, and she was always gay and willing to be jolly with us. Aunt Jane was tall and angular, and almost too good, we thought, for human nature's daily food. It was with the best intentions, I am sure, that she prayed aloud for us by name at one of her meetings. Both of the aunts were kindness itself to us.

Uncle Willie, who liked to describe himself in Sir Walter Scott's phrase as ' a just-leevin' man for a country writer,' was one of the most delightful people I have ever known. As a small child I wondered if he could be a relation of the parrot. They had both hooked noses and rather tight eyes, and when Uncle Willie stood before the parrot's cage, dancing and singing :

> " Merrily danced the Quaker's wife,
> And merrily danced the Quaker . . ."

and the parrot imitated him, the likeness to me seemed quite absurd. My father was fair and blue-eyed, but with his pale face and dark eyes and small black beard, Uncle Willie looked almost like a foreigner. ' Equable, alert and gay,' no one enjoyed the good things of life better than he. His hobby was French history and literature and he spent most of his holidays in France. That spring when Willie and Walter had gone back to college he and Aunt Kate took me to Paris for a holiday. It was not, of course, my first experience of what the Golden Age children called ' that beastly abroad,' but Paris I had only passed through, and to be there with someone who knew it intimately was a privilege. Even more interesting was to stay at Tours, and visit the châteaux of the Loire. Then history was made too interesting to be resisted.

Willie's vacation that summer had to be a very busy one,

as he had both his I.C.S. exams and ' Greats ' before him,
so he elected to stay at a moorland farm where two of our
uncles had their home, and where he would have no temp-
tation to waste precious time. He got up at six every
morning and had a swim in the pond before breakfast, then
worked hard all day. Walter and I stayed at Broughton
Green and often walked the four miles to have tea with
him, but he could never be persuaded to spare us more
than half an hour. At Broughton Green there was now
only gentle ' Antaggie ' and our youngest uncle. Our
grandmother had ruled everyone with her strong personality and without her the house had a somewhat relaxed
air. Now we could do or say anything we pleased, but
instead of feeling it a relief we were conscious of loss :
something was gone that could not be replaced, and we
missed it.

In July the Bible Christians who had been living in our
house in Glasgow wrote that they had got orders to return
to America, and Walter and I decided to go and see in what
state they had left the house. We had heard some queer
tales from people in the neighbourhood of meetings held
and cures performed, and we wondered.

Two of the tenants were waiting to deliver up the house
to us, and we had a talk with them about their work. Evidently they regarded themselves as being in the Apostolic
succession, and believed that they could cure by the laying
on of hands. They seemed quite honest in their belief,
and said they had had some wonderful results. Seeing our
dubious faces, they said naïvely that perhaps they ought
not to have held meetings in a private house, but they
had asked God not to let the carpets be any the worse.

It looked as if the prayer had been answered, the carpets
did not look any the worse, but, knowing how Mother
would hate the thought that perhaps infectious cases had

been in the house, we decided to start at once and clean it.

I had often seen the house cleaned, and helped in small ways, but to tackle it ourselves was something of an undertaking. We started at the top, taking a room at a time. Everything that would wash was sent to the laundry, and carpets were taken away to be beaten by machinery. Meantime we swept down the walls, beat the furniture, and polished all the pictures. My job was the scrubbing of the floors, and I put so much soda into the water that they positively glistened, and my hands were a wreck for weeks after. So pleased were we with the result of our labours that we thought we would continue the good work and whitewash the basement. That was a test of endurance, but we made some sort of a job and were rewarded by the refreshed look of the place.

In Elizabethan days they had a good name for the spring-cleaning—the sweetening. Our 'sweetening' took us a whole week, working from dawn till dusk. Little time was spent on meals. Breakfast was rolls and boiled eggs; lunch, tinned tongue and new potatoes and tarts; supper consisted of what was left.

For the first time in my life I felt I had accomplished something, done a real job of work, but without the good-natured Walter it could not have been done at all.

When the wanderers had returned and we were together again at Broughton, Mother said:

"I wonder what the poor old house is like! The cleaning will be a big job."

With what pride I said carelessly:

"Oh, that's all right. Walter and I cleaned it."

They brought home from South Africa the most wonderful assortment of presents given them by various kind people: dozens of ostrich feathers, a Kaross, a great Kaffir basket full of gifts, not to speak of jars of amusing jams, and wonderful dried fruit. The Mhor had acquired, as well as a strong colonial accent, an enormous tortoise, which lived for many years contentedly in the Green garden.

The travellers could not say enough about the kindness they had met with, and the hospitality received. Naturally, what interested us most was to hear of the time John had spent with them.

J. B. stayed for about two years with Lord Milner, and ever afterwards South Africa had a warm corner of his heart. His book *Prester John* is dedicated to Lionel Phillips in these words :

> " Time, they say, must the best of us capture,
>   And travel and battle and gems and gold
> No more can kindle the ancient rapture,
>   For even the youngest of hearts grows old.
> But in you, I think, the boy is not over ;
>   So take this medley of ways and wars
> As the gift of a friend and a fellow-lover
>   Of the fairest country under the stars."

He returned home in September 1903. We had taken a farm-house called Altarstone, standing on the banks of the Tweed above Stobo, and a large family party welcomed him there. That time seems impregnated with the tune of ' Waltzing Matilda.' John had heard the Australian soldiers singing it and brought it to us, and someone was always shouting :

> " You come a-waltzing, Matilda, Matilda."

It is odd to hear it again in this war.

We shouted other things as well. It was a good thing there was no one near enough to be disturbed, for every night the welkin rang with our voices uplifted in every song we knew. Anyone hearing us might have thought we were too convivial a gathering, but we were drunk only with the wine of youth and the joy of being together.

In another year Willie sailed for India, having passed high into the Indian Civil Service. We had long dreaded his departure. Willie had a stormy childhood and grew into a most pugnacious schoolboy. He was constantly fighting, and almost every day came home from school with buttons torn from his coat and other marks of conflict. Mother sometimes asked despairingly what was to happen to such a boy, but Father only laughed, and said :

" Let him alone : he'll be the best of the lot yet."

Willie believed in not letting the sun go down upon his wrath. He had to go to sleep at peace with everyone. He would say to Walter with whom he shared a room :

" Have I hit you to-day ? Well, I'm sorry. Say you forgive me or I'll hit you again."

No one could help liking him, he was so far from cunning and so utterly honest. When he was about fifteen he suddenly woke to an interest in his lessons, began to look forward, and made up his mind he would enter the Indian Civil Service, and he never turned back.

His first district was Barisal. He wrote :

" The Collector is a Herculean Scot called Beatson-Bell, son of a Sheriff of Fife. He says the district is not malarial at all. You can get excellent and very cheap polo, and the best of sport—anything from a tiger to a snipe. It is much more important to have a good Collector than a good district, and B. B. is one of the keenest officers in the service."

After a year at Barisal Willie served successively as Assistant Magistrate in Chapra and Subdivisional Officer in Gopalganj and Gobindpur. He then entered the Secretariat as Under-Secretary and remained there till January

1908, when he was appointed Registrar of Agricultural Banks, a post which he held until July 1912, when he came home on leave.

He was always keen about his work, but in ' Banks,' one of his friends wrote, he found his *métier*. He made himself a specialist on all forms of Agricultural Co-operation, and not only did valuable work for his Department, but prepared a number of careful and authoritative reports on special points.

In spite of ' black dividing sea and alien plain ' his heart was always at home.

" Mother seems to think," he wrote in 1906, " that I am losing interest in the family. If she knew how much I think about you all she wouldn't say that. I am simply living for my leave. It is grand to think that *this* year I may get home."

Long before his leave was sanctioned he had engaged a berth, and given us elaborate instruction about writing to different ports.

" I have got a cabin on the hurricane deck of the *Caledonia*, and shall make the unwarrantable assumption that nothing will come in the way of my leave and direct your future correspondence accordingly. . . . All this is subject to your getting no letter or cable saying my leave is postponed. Don't count on my leave, but brace yourselves up to the possibility. I think I should like to spend a good deal of the time in Peeblesshire. I have great yearnings for those green hills."

Before his first leave came, Uncle Willie died.

" I have just returned from Purulia and found your letter with its terribly sad news of Uncle Willie's death. I hadn't realised he was so ill and the news was a great shock. He was a fine man, and the kindest I ever knew. He will make a great gap in all our lives. If I can look back on as 'just-leevin'' an existence as his when my time comes I shall be content."

Willie's first leave was only three months, about six weeks at home, but it was enough, he said, to build the bridge. We found him quite unchanged, the same kind, simple boy, eager to spend his money buying presents for everyone, determined to pay for every treat. Then of course, his money went done. I remember one evening how he lay on the floor with a piece of paper and a pencil trying to find out if he had any money to go back with.

Uncle Willie's death changed things. Walter, who had hoped to go to the Scots Bar, had to take up the family business in Peebles, and became a writer and banker, and procurator fiscal and town clerk. He was very young and with no experience, so it was rather a large handling. I was sent to keep house for him, as the two aunts had decided to make their home in Guernsey. So life changed for me too.

John, meantime, had given up the Bar and had settled down in London as a director in the publishing firm of Thomas Nelson & Sons. He was, I think, the prime mover in starting cheap reprints of well-known books. Nelson's ' Sevenpennies,' well bound and well printed, became very popular.

It was about this time that he decided that I ought to have some money of my own and gave me an allowance of £100 a year. I thought then, and I think now, that it was a remarkable thing for a young man to do. But it gave him pleasure, I believe, and it made all the difference in the world to me; to have a cheque-book of my own made me feel like a millionaire. Even when I no longer needed it he could hardly be persuaded to give it up.

CHAPTER VII

"The heavens forbid
But that our loves and comforts should increase
Even as our days do grow."

Othello.

IT was in the winter of 1906 that John told us he hoped to marry Susan Grosvenor. This was an event of great importance to us as a family, to Mother more especially, and she was inclined a little to dread the changes it would bring. As for me, ' a long time ago the world began,' and since the world's beginning John had been my playmate, my comrade, my counsellor. To him I owed so much of the pleasure and interest in my life that I very earnestly wished him well.

In January 1907 Mother and I went to London, to Brown's Hotel, to make Susan's acquaintance. It was something of an ordeal for us to meet for the first time one who would mean a great deal in our lives, but infinitely worse for Susie (as she was always called) to enter so close-knit a family as ours.

But, happily, she had always lived in an atmosphere of strong family affection, and that made her very understanding. It was a busy and amusing time, a round of luncheons and dinners and plays and meeting interesting people.

The other day, when turning out cupboards for salvage I found, carefully put away, some things that brought back a forgotten occasion—a silver bell (made of cardboard), a tiny silver slipper, and a crumbling spray of what had been white heather, tied with a silver ribbon. They were relics of a betrothal party given for the young couple by the Ecksteins, in their house in Park Lane. They had known John in Johannesburg, and had collected everyone

103

then in London connected with that time, including Lord Milner. The table, I remember, was very bridal, with a great bell of white flowers in the middle, the menu was printed on silver bells, silver slippers held sweets, and the food was practically all white. One almost expected the footmen to be got up as cupids.

After dinner a crowd of people came in. The person I was most interested in was Sarah Macnaughtan, whose books, *Christina McNab* and *The Expensive Miss du Cane*, I had much enjoyed. She was delightfully easy to talk to and we made friends at once, and there and then she invited me to stay with her when the wedding came off.

I had a talk with Lord Milner. It was rather a fearful pleasure, but having John in common made things easier.

In the spring Susie came to visit us in Peebles. She confessed later that she had come prepared with subjects of conversation for each of us. To Mother (knowing her interest in social work) she was going to talk of ' the poor.' Father was to have flowers and Walter poetry.

One of the things that drew Susie and me together was a habit we shared of becoming convulsed with helpless, painful laughter at the most inopportune moments. It was generally at public meetings that we behaved in this disgraceful way. Once, when we were sitting trying to look like serious politicians on the platform of a Unionist meeting, a good, earnest worker from Ulster said, " The grocer in our village is a viper," whereupon we had each a vision of a Home Rule viper standing on its tail, dealing out sugar and flour—and we were lost.

The most trivial thing betrayed us. When a certain well-known woman opened her speech on Women's Suffrage with the statement, " I am not very *au fait* with matters at Budapest," we glanced at each other with the question in our eyes, " *Why* Budapest ? " and then dissolved.

The wedding took place at St. George's, Hanover Square, in July 1907. I was one of eight bridesmaids, all relations, all dressed in pink and silver and carrying silver baskets of sweet-peas.

Mother bought her wedding hat in the middle of a bad thunderstorm and said that it always gave her a solemnised feeling to put it on!

Willie wrote:

" I wish your letters wouldn't go round by Darjeeling; I was looking forward very much to your last to hear about J. B.'s wedding and it didn't come till yesterday. I saw portraits of the misguided couple in several of the papers. Shortly after the mail came in I got a note from Lady Fraser bidding me to dinner that night. She had made a collection of photos and references to the wedding, and had asked me simply to show them to me. Wasn't it kind? . . . I perceive you were dressed in *ninon-de-soie*. Never heard of it. But John said you looked beautiful. Surely that wasn't possible? . . . What a gay gallivantin' family you are! And my elderly respectable father kissing his daughter-in-law and jaunting over to Paris! He'll be losing his job one of these days . . ."

Had I not been so rich in brothers I might have felt a little forlorn when the couple departed to climb in the Dolomites. But it had always been a plan that some day I should visit Willie in India, and he now wrote that he very much wanted me to come that autumn. He had a job in the Secretariat that would keep him in Calcutta for several months, which, he thought, would be more interesting for me than a country station, so it was arranged that I should sail in October.

There is an old Scots saying, *There's muckle adae when cadgers ride*, and we had a hectic time preparing for my departure. Piles of washing frocks were needed, garden-party clothes, evening-dresses (one specially smart for the Drawing-Room at Government House), as well as travelling things and riding kit.

I was divided between delight at the thought of seeing Willie (and the wonders of India) and deepest dejection at leaving everyone else. When I went to say good-bye to an invalid girl who spent her days lying in the kitchen bed of a house in a tenement down by the Clyde, she wanted to hear all about my new dresses, and said wistfully, " Your life's just like a fairy tale." It was a new idea to me and made me think.

Mother and John and Susie saw me off at Tilbury on a day of rain and gloom, and I was introduced to some friends of the Grosvenors who were going to Egypt, and who arranged that I should sit with them at the Captain's table.

There were three of us in our cabin : one I can't remember much about except that she insisted on keeping in the cabin a large square hat-box which was a rock of offence and a stumbling-block all through the voyage : the other was called Gladys Helder, ' G.' to me. It would be impossible to imagine a nicer person for a cabin companion. Not only was she was white and pink and golden as a morning in May—even sea-sickness did not make her look plain—but she had a delightful disposition. What the voyage would have been like without her I can't think, for long before Ushant had slammed the door on us we were prone on our backs, our world bounded by the four walls of the cabin and damp handkerchiefs under our pillows to testify to the depressed state of our minds. I couldn't even read any of the books I had with me except, now and again, a page or two of *Memories and Portraits* : there was a certain comfort in reading of such steady quiet places as the Pentland Hills and the decent men who do their herding there.

In time we got our sea legs (though we were liable at

the slightest roll to lose them again) and we enjoyed greatly
the days on shore ! Port Said, where we bought *topis* and
Turkish Delight ; Colombo, where we rode in rickshaws
to the Galle Face Hotel and tasted for the first time real
curry.

We talked together endlessly, G. and I. She was going
to Calcutta to spend the cold weather with her sister, and
we earnestly hoped we might be near each other. Willie
was returning from Darjeeling only a day or two before
our boat arrived, and knowing my casual brother, I thought
it quite likely that our lodging would be the cold ground.

After a breathless night in the Hoogly we got into the
Kidderpore Docks. G. and I, up betimes, clad in clean
white frocks to meet the burning, shining face of India,
found all the people who had come to meet the boat penned
like sheep in an enclosure. Presently they were allowed on
board, and in a few minutes Willie and I were clutching
each other, G. had found her sister, and all was well.

The special providence that looks after casual people
had guided Willie to a comfortable boarding-house in
Russel Street. It was not at all my idea of a boarding-house,
consisting as it did of four large houses, all standing a
little apart in a compound. They were let out in suites of
rooms, and the occupants fed together in the public dining-
room. We had four rooms on the ground floor, a sort of
drawing-room, a study, and two bedrooms. Willie's bedroom was next his study, but I had to take a walk outside
to reach mine. Like all the rooms it was high and white-
washed, and the really disturbing thing—there were ten
different ways of entering it, doors and windows, all guilt-
less of lock or bar. When we walked round together to
inspect it that first day we found all my trunks, and, sitting
among them, my ayah, a small person wrapped in a white
' *sari*,' with demure shy eyes and teeth stained red with

chewing betel-nut. She called me Missy-baba, I called her Bella.

It seemed odd that, living in a sort of hotel, we should need such troops of servants. Willie's bearer, who took entire charge of us both, and whom we christened Pagett, M.P., because of his fondness for making speeches ; my ayah, a *kitmutgar* or butler to wait on us at table and bring tea in the afternoon ; a young assistant *kitmutgar* ; a small boy who rejoiced in the name of *pani-wallah* (whose sole duty was to carry water for our baths) ; a *dhobi* who washed our clothes ; and a *syce* for each pony. Seated as we sometimes saw them in rows on the steps, augmented by a Government *chuprassi* or two in brilliant uniforms, they made a sufficiently imposing spectacle.

Having no Hindustani I could not speak to them, but I looked at them as pleasantly as I knew how because I didn't want them to mutiny or do anything desperate, but Willie discouraged me at the outset, saying : " You needn't grin at them so affably, they'll only think you weak in the head."

Except at breakfast and in the evenings I never saw Willie. Up every morning at six o'clock, he had nearly three hours' work done before breakfast. At 9.30 he left for the office, the *kitmutgar* carrying some sandwiches and a bottle of soda-water, which was his modest lunch. Sometimes he got home for tea, and we would have a drive in the Maidan, or a ride on the racecourse, or a game at tennis. If we were at home for dinner, we sat and talked for a bit, then he went to his study and worked till midnight, for all day long *chuprassis* flitted in and out, piling his table with documents marked Urgent.

Fortunately G. was quite near and always came along after breakfast to spend the morning with me, and her sister, Mrs. Turner, made me welcome at any time. She

and her husband had a great airy house, charmingly furnished, standing in a large garden. When Willie had to
go suddenly to the Mofussil for a week, they actually
furnished an empty room next G.'s, that she and I might
be together. There was no end to their kindness.

G. was a great success in Calcutta. A first-class tennis
player, good at all games, loving dancing and fun, she was
well fitted for the life, and her sister was very proud of her.

Having heard so much about Anglo-Indian women we
were somewhat nervous of encountering them. Mrs.
Hawksbee of the acid tongue and good heart we frequently
met and recognised, but ladies who ' fibbed with subtle
venom ' we were lucky enough to escape. I don't see why
they should exist in India more than any other place.

In 1771, when young Thackeray arrived in India with
his two sisters, Henrietta and Jane, his mother predicted,
" If there's a sensible man in India he will find out Jane " ;
and it seemed to me that there must be no lack of sensible
men in India, so many had been fortunate in finding kind,
gentle, unaffected wives. A few of the women we definitely
disliked, but only a few.

Calcutta itself interested me greatly, and I found its
history fascinating. The chapter in *The Thackerays in India*
on ' Some Calcutta Graves ' made me long to find the Park
Street Cemetery, but G. refused curtly to have anything
to do with such a quest, pointing out that it was bad enough
to be living in such a sudden and dangerous land without
going to look for cemeteries.

Not even the prospect of seeing the stone bearing the
name of Rose Aylmer, Walter Savage Landor's first love,
moved her. I told her the pitiful story as I knew it. She
had fallen in love with the penniless young poet, so her
people sent her out to Calcutta to her aunt, Lady Russel,
and there she died at the age of twenty.

> " ' Her noble name she never changed,' (wrote Landor),
> ' Nor was her noble heart estranged.' "

and in his sorrow he wrote the poem, " which," says the writer of the book, " enshrines in a casket of pearl the name of Rose Aylmer, as long as maiden hearts shall ache, and the English language last."

> " Ah what avails the sceptred race ?
> Ah what the form divine ?
> What every virtue, every grace ?
> Rose Aylmer, all were thine."

But all G. said was, " You and your cemeteries ! "

There was a lot of entertaining in Calcutta, and I was glad of all my evening-dresses. Willie had a bad habit of coming too close behind me when we were being ushered into a room and treading on my tail. One pale-green satin dress that I particularly liked had a long train, and when I wore it we were generally announced to the sound of gathers rending.

Not being very sociably inclined we really preferred dining together alone. It seemed to amaze and amuse our fellow-boarders that a brother and sister should have so much to say to each other, and find so much reason for mirth.

" *Listen* to the little Buchans laughing," they would say.

Every now and again we had to give a dinner. At first I protested that we had no silver and nothing to make the table look decent.

" Leave it to the servants," I was told. " It'll be all right."

So I engaged the private dining-room and left it. The servants were worthy of their trust; the table looked charming. I had never seen any of the things before, but I rather feared the guests probably had.

When Kipling wrote his *Christmas in India*, I think he must have been in a dâk-bungalow, down with fever, otherwise he would hardly have painted such a gloomy picture. I found it a very agreeable time, full of gaiety and good cheer, but then, as was pointed out to me, I was only a cold-weather visitor! India was not my 'grim stepmother.'

The great event of the Christmas season was our visit to Darjeeling. To see the Himalayas was one of my most cherished ambitions, and Willie felt he must spare a week-end to take me there.

The journey itself was full of interest and novelty! crossing the Ganges on a ferry-boat that had a dinner-table laid out on deck, decorated for Christmas with branches, Chinese lanterns, and large deadly-looking iced cakes.

At Siliguri everything, surprisingly, was glittering with frost, and the few natives seen about had their heads wrapped up in shawls as if they were suffering from tooth-ache. The toy-train on the Darjeeling-Himalaya railway was waiting; a man banged on a bit of metal by way of a bell, and we set off on our journey to cloudland, and cloud-land it was when we arrived at Darjeeling, bitterly cold, so that we were glad to get into the hotel and find fires blazing in our bedrooms.

On Sunday it was still misty, but Willie held out hopes that it would clear.

It was market-day, and the village street was lined on both sides with booths, and thronged with people, jolly-looking squat little men and women, hung with silver chains and wearing heavy earrings set with turquoises, their faces puckered with laughing. I was buying some lumps of rough turquoise when Willie suddenly gripped my arm. I looked straight across the valley.

"Higher," said Willie, and I lifted my eyes literally to

the skies, and there—suddenly—behold—beyond—were the everlasting snows, Kangchenjunga towering in ' valorous isolation.'

That alone was worth going to India to see. We were particularly interested in the Himalayas at that time, for Willie's great friend, Cecil Rawling, had just come back from exploring the sources of the Brahmaputra, and they had planned to write a history of Tibet together. I listened to much talk of this project when Captain Rawling came to dine with us, as he often did, in Calcutta. He had a passion for strange lands, and later on explored Dutch New Guinea, discovered a new pigmy race, and was awarded the Royal Geographical Society's Founder's Medal. John made his acquaintance when he and Willie were both in London in 1909, and they became friends, and planned great schemes together. The war put a stop to these, and Cecil Rawling was killed in 1917, in France.

In the end of December Willie got a new job—Registrar of Banks—which meant that he would have to start almost at once on a tour of inspection in the Mofussil. (When I heard first the Mofussil mentioned I supposed it was some sort of prophet, but found it only meant the country districts.)

Before we left, G. and I were presented at the Drawing-Room at Government House, and enjoyed a Fancy Dress Ball at the same place.

It was sad to say good-bye to G. and her sister for a couple of months, and to all the kind people who had made my stay in Calcutta so pleasant, not to speak of our fellow-guests in what Willie vulgarly called ' the hash-house,' but it was tremendously exciting to think of going about with Willie and seeing something of the real India.

It was decided to leave my ayah in Calcutta. Pagett, of course, must go, and the *syces* with the ponies. (Willie thought there might be a chance of polo, and, anyway, Pagett wanted them to go; he said it made the Sahib look more important!)

All the money we had with us travelled in a box among the luggage. I was aghast, but was told it was the ' correct idear.'

Starting on this trek was rather like *The Young Visiters*. I felt akin to Ethèl Monticue, who ' did not really know at all how to go on a trip,' and to Mr. Salteena, who said, ' I shall wear my white alpaka coat to keep off the dust and flies. I hope I shall enjoy myself."

Railway stations are very much a feature of life in India. At all times the native loves travelling, and as he has no notion of time-tables, often arrives at the station the night before, sleeps peacefully on the ground, and is in comfortable time for the first train in the morning. Also, he has no idea of fixed charges, and when he goes to the ticket-office to ask for his ' tickut,' and the babu in charge tells him the price, he offers half. When that is refused he goes away, and returns in an hour or so to offer a little more. It may take a whole day to convince him that he can't beat down the railway company. As it happened, when we started on our tour there was a great festival going on which only happens once in a very long time. If they bathe in the holy Ganges while this festival is going on, they believe that all their sins are washed away. They came flocking from all parts, eagerly boarding every train that stopped, regardless of the direction it was going in, and I greatly fear many of the poor people must have missed that chance of salvation.

After a night and a day in a train, we got out at quite an important station, where the refreshment-room had a table laid for dinner, and tall glass cases round the walls filled with all sorts of tinned meats, biscuits, butter, and jam, for in the Mofussil provisions are bought at the railway station. We had a meal, and Willie produced a pencil and paper, and we made out a list of what we thought we would need, and saw them packed in a wooden box.

It was then about eight o'clock in the evening, and I asked when our train was due. Four a.m., I was told. " Where are we to sleep ? " I asked.

Willie waved his hand. " Anywhere. Let's see what the waiting-room's like."

It was like nothing on earth, a large, dirty, barnlike apartment, with cane seats arranged round the walls ; one small lamp smelling vilely served to make darkness visible : an aged crone crouched in one corner.

Pagett took up my roll of bedding and laid it out on a seat, and in that dreary and far from clean apartment, with horrible insects walking up the walls, and doubtless carpeting the floor, I slept dreamlessly. Willie spent the night in the refreshment-room. Pagett had gone to the station-master, demanded a bed for a First Class Commissioner-Sahib, and, so far does impudence carry one, got it.

I learned much on that tour of dâk-bungalows (rest-houses where travellers can stay for a little), and dirty, dreary places many of them were, but in some ways preferable to a tent. It is awful to wake up in a tent in the middle of the night and hear a jackal yell, and feel certain that a tiger must be padding stealthily towards one ; to have no door to lock and know that there is nothing but a mosquito-curtain between one and a fearful end is rather unnerving.

Willie laughed, calling me a *funkstick*, and gave me a *chokidar* to sleep beside my tent, but he turned out to be such an utterly villainous-looking creature that one felt the jackal—or even the tiger—was the ' more natural beast of the twain.'

As Willie was away most of the day, doing long treks on his bicycle in the heat, I had many hours alone, but I was never bored, indeed, I felt myself becoming exactly like a native, sitting contentedly doing nothing but look before me for hours. Of course I wrote innumerable letters, and it occurred to me that it would be fun to make a book of them to keep as a memento of my experiences. So, with that object before me, I noted down things people told me, and anything I saw that struck me as interesting or amusing.

It was an odd but very peaceful life. One became accustomed to jungly cooking, and dishes washed behind the tent in water that was positively thick, and dried with a cloth that had begun life cleaning our brown shoes! It was a great mistake, I found, to enquire into things that we were not intended to see.

We did not always live in squalor. Sometimes we were near a station where we were royally entertained, dined in our smartest clothes, danced, and attended polo matches. The kindness we received was immense. Once we stayed a week with a most delightful family to whom we became so attached that we could hardly bear to leave.

Sometimes we found in a dâk-bungalow a cook who gave us what Pagett called ' Calcutta dinners,' and sometimes we got no dinner at all and ate ginger-snaps. Nothing like that mattered to us ; we were together and happy.

One very pleasant thing about that nomadic life was that we got nearer to the people. They came in the evenings, in little groups, to talk to Willie outside his tent, and I saw how patient he was with them, how anxious to help. They made my heart ache, those country people ; they were so gentle and so desperately poor. Was it Stevens who said that the Indian ryot has been starving for twenty centuries and sees no reason why he should ever be filled ?

The evening in camp was the loveliest time, when Willie's long day was over and we sat together watching the wood-smoke hanging in wisps in the still air, and listened to the conches from the temple, and the song of the boys bringing the cattle home, while the sunset colours faded into the deep blue of the Indian night.

It was very hot when we got back to Calcutta, and I found a big airy bedroom with a bathroom, and an ayah to look after my clothes, a pleasant change from the cramped space of a tent, a zinc bath wiggling on an uneven floor, and Pagett fumbling vaguely among my belongings.

My passage had been taken on the *Simla*, sailing in the end of March, and I was rejoiced to hear that G. was again to be my cabin companion. It had been intended that she should stay on for the summer and go to the hills, but she told me, " D'you think I would let you get away home and leave me here ? Not likely ! "

Mother had written begging me to bring some stuff for a sale of work, and we had a hectic time collecting things.

It was possible to get good brass in the villages, lotas and platters that were very decorative. When the *chicon-wallah* paid a visit and spread his wares on the verandah floor we got rugs from Kashmir, tinsel-embroidered mats, pieces of soft, bright silk, and white sewed work. Down in the city was the China Bazaar, where we rooted about, unearthing treasures in the way of old brass vases, queer slender-necked scent bottles still smelling faintly of roses, old lacquer boxes, bits of rich embroidery, not to speak of candlesticks and trays and silver-work.

It was a miserable business leaving Willie. Mr. Turner

had by some means managed to get permission for himself and his wife and Willie to go down the river in the launch that took passengers to the *Simla*. On board we all had breakfast together at the Captain's table, and almost immediately after our people had to go back, and G. and I, very stricken, watched the launch steam up the river till it was lost to sight.

Willie wrote the night we left :

" I felt a miserable and rather lonely creature as your face faded into the distance, and the old black *Simla* hid itself round a bend in the river. When I got back your ayah was there waiting for her pay. When she got it she remarked, ' Missy-baba very good missy-baba, she was never angry with me ! ' So your tip didn't fail to work. She wanted to know when you were coming back and was led away comfortless by Pagett, who explained in a lofty tone that the Miss-Sahib had only come to inspect the country. Then I went to my office and drowned my sorrows in hard work, which is a wonderful antidote to home-sickness.

" It is really a mistake for a family to be too affectionate. It is too unsettling. I am missing you horribly, so I ought to be a very efficient member of the administration till I grow reconciled to a solitary existence again. Write very long letters to me. When you get this you will be west of Suez with the terrors of the Red Sea behind you ; and the East will seem a dream that is past. In the atmosphere of the West it ought to be rather a pleasant dream, but I think you enjoyed the reality too. You will read this at the parting of the East and West. To the time-expired service man and the Eastern visitor it ought to be a place of regrets. To me it is the beginning of all that is most delightful to dream about. Many a time I think of that turning into the Mediterranean and the boat heading towards clean cold Western lands. Not because I'm un-happy in India, only it is part of our existence always to be dreaming of the only country. Tweedside and those green hills will be all the nicer, and more stable, with the theatrical Orient for a background."

CHAPTER VIII

" . . . Honour and praise he asked not : fame in the sun
  Ne'er vexed his thought ; nay, even the city of gold
He would forego if haply, by his loss,
  His wearied sheep might safely come to fold.
He was content to hold the world as dross,
  And thereby all things won.
Toiling, he found the balm nought mortal yields ;
  He drew from poverty fulness, joy from pain ;
Scattering full-handed, reaped he ample fields ;
  To him to live was Christ—to die was gain."

J. B.

THE voyage from India was all pleasure. The *Simla* was a small boat and the passengers were mostly soldiers going home to their families, some on leave, others for good, and some young men who had been making a tour of the East. Everyone seemed in the best of spirits, and we were all very friendly together. As G. and I were almost the only girls on board we had a very good time and were sincerely sorry when the voyage ended.

We remained close friends. G. married very happily in 1916, and had two children. I was godmother to the boy. Gordon was a godson to be proud of. He did wonders at Charterhouse and Cambridge, and had just sailed for Burma to his first job when his mother died, to the great grief of all who knew her. She was spared the anxiety of the months of silence after the Jap invasion, but she missed the joy of hearing of her boy's[1] safe arrival in India.

Susie's first baby, a girl, was born in the June after I got home. John wrote, " A daughter is a great interest," and we were all anxious to see our new relation. We did see her in July, when Walter took us all for a holiday to Zermatt, and we stopped in London going and coming back.

[1] Reported missing, believed killed, in May 1944.

The next summer Willie came home for his second leave. He had about three months at home. John took a farm-house with some rough shooting among the Meldon Hills, Harehope by name. It was a good holiday place, for though only a few miles from Peebles it was quite in the wilds; it was a very happy summer. Baby Alice was a great delight and amusement, especially to the Mhor (whom we now began to call by his proper name, Alastair), who was the most admiring of boy uncles.

At Harehope Susie and Willie got to know each other, and became great friends. She was much struck by the way he worked, even on holiday, at the history he was writing. No lovely weather or tempting sport lured him away from his morning's work. She liked the way he laughed at himself and took everything that happened with the same humorous philosophy, whether it was missing an easy shot or losing a game.

All too soon his leave was over, but before he left he made us promise that we would insist on Father retiring. We had noticed that his step was slower, and that he some-times said that he was beginning to be afraid of that which was high, and wondered, laughing, why his people liked to live at the very top of the tallest tenements, but we did not confess even to ourselves that he was failing. He was only just over sixty, but the hard life of a city minister had worn him out.

At first Father scouted the idea of giving up his work; he felt he would be deserting people who depended on him, and it took two specialists to convince him that it was necessary.

Walter and I were settled in the old house on the bridge, and we found a house for the parents on the hill just across Tweed Bridge. It had belonged to an artist, and there was a large room opening on the garden that had been used as

MY FATHER, THE REV. JOHN BUCHAN.

a studio. It made a splendid study, and Father had all his books round him, and the garden, in which he intended to make great improvements, at hand. The removal had been got over, the house had already a home-like look, and Anne-from-Skye (who had succeeded Marget) seemed inclined to like life at Peebles, so all was well, and we began to prepare for a holiday in Switzerland.

Since Violet's death we had enjoyed years of health and prosperity. So well did things seem to work out for us that people talked of 'the Buchan luck,' and I used to look pityingly at people on whom blow after blow fell, and wonder how they bore up at all. But few people get off unscathed, and our turn came.

On the day we started on our holiday Father looked rather tired, and before we reached London confessed to having a pain in his chest. John was dining with us at the Grosvenor, and telephoned for his own doctor who, when he had made an examination, said that Father must on no account travel. Walter and Alastair and I stayed on at the Grosvenor while the parents went to John's house in Bryanston Street. Father improved in a day or two and began to worry about Walter missing his holiday, so to please him the three of us crossed to France.

Happily we went no further than Paris, for the next day we got a wire telling us to come back at once as Father was very ill. It was a bad heart attack, and though he recovered from it, the doctors warned us that it might occur at any time, and that he must lead the quietest life with no work or hurry or excitement, and no walking except on the level.

It was a blow to him, for he had hoped in his leisure to help so many people, but he accepted it with a good grace, and managed to make of his restricted life something spacious and serene. It was a joy to him to be back in

Peebles, and able to take short walks through the fields
he had played in as a boy, and feast his eyes on the hills
he could no longer climb, to wander in the garden and
note his special plants ; to come in and write a chapter of
his book, ' Peeblesshire Poets ' ; to read, sometimes, his
little brown Baxter's *Saints' Rest*, or some story of high
adventure, or his beloved Sir Walter ; to enjoy the family
life, and laugh like a boy at the foolish family jests. Some
of the men who had been boys when he was a boy were still
in the town. One of them, a notorious poacher—who in
his sober senses passed his one-time companion with
averted head—if he had had rather much to drink would
greet him jovially with a " Man, John, d'you mind yon big
yin in the pool up Soonhope ? "

It was a good thing Father was fairly well, because
Mother's health was giving us anxiety. She was being
treated for anæmia, when she suddenly began to take bouts
of fever ; to all appearances quite well, she would shiver
violently, and before we could get her upstairs and into
bed she was delirious, with a temperature of 106. There
seemed to be nothing we could do to ward off these turns,
and they were a constant menace. It was so disappointing
for her to get up her strength and be well enough to be
downstairs, only to be thrown back.

She would say, " I'm at the foot of the precipice again,"
but she never lost her spirit.

It was a dreadful time, for no doctor seemed to know
what was causing the fever. I often wished that Mother
had been one of those women who seem positively to
enjoy being ill and like having visits from doctors, but,
like the boy in *The Golden Age*, she held the sacred art of
healing in horror and contempt, and nurses she had no
use for.

We had a very nice middle-aged one, but she had an

unfortunate taste for repeating poetry, and would try to soothe her patient off to sleep with

"The stag at e'en had drunk its fill . . ."

and that stag so got on Mother's nerves that I had to beg her to desist.

What a blessing that even in times of dire distress and anxiety there is always something to laugh at! Well or ill, Mother could not help being a comic. As Alastair said, trying not to cry, when the doctor told us he hardly thought she would live through the night, "If she weren't such a *funny* wee body!"

If Mother was rather a resentful patient, there was little of the ministering angel about me as a nurse. She complained that I shied hot-water bags into her bed, and there was truth in the accusation, but I had a lot on my head.

We had shut up the house that we had put right with so much pleasure in the spring, and all that winter the family lived with Walter. When Mother was able to take an interest in what was going on she would ask me searching questions about the servants, if everything was being done regularly, and about the housekeeping books, then would remark sadly that she feared there was a great leakage. I am sure there was, but I had neither my Mother's cleverness nor her experience, and was thankful simply to keep things going. The anxiety was very bad for Father, and we had to try to keep him as calm as possible. It was hard, too, on Alastair, with his horror of sadness, those recurrent crises, and in the holidays he just went about the house kicking things. Often Walter and I had to take turns of sitting up several nights in succession, as we did not care to leave Mother alone with a nurse when she was unconscious, and to pass the time and keep myself awake, I got out the MSS. I was writing about my experiences in

India. It was an escape from the unhappy present to go back into the sunshine of light-hearted days.

In the spring (1911) we felt something must be done. John had heard of Sir Almroth Wright, and thought we should bring Mother to London to see him. It seemed a great risk, but we decided to take it. Walter could be trusted to see that Father was well looked after, and we had two thoroughly good maids, so one morning in March Mother and I set off. We were going to Great-uncle John's house, alone now with Maud Mark, and that was like a second home to us all.

John was waiting at Euston, miserably wondering if an ambulance would be required, but Mother could always be relied on to play up in an emergency. There she was, smiling at him and saying she had enjoyed the journey.

Of course she paid for it. Two days later she went down with one of the worst bouts of fever that she had had, and in it Sir Almroth Wright saw her. We had been expecting a London doctor, very smart, with a manner, and it was extraordinarily comforting to see this tall, rather stooped man, with a somewhat shabby overcoat, who told us he had a mother of his own whom he would hate to lose. Later on he told John he had discovered what was wrong with Mother (some sort of germ attacking the blood), but whether she could be cured was doubtful.

We went to his house every four days for inoculation. It was too soon to say the treatment was doing good, but the change helped Mother, being in new surroundings, seeing different people. She had been kept on a very low diet, but Sir Almroth said she might eat anything, the more the better, and she enjoyed that. Maud was a wonderful stand-by. She got up herself very early (knowing that Mother slept badly), and appeared with a tempting break-fast tray.

In April Walter took his holiday. He and Alastair stayed at the Grosvenor, and Father came beside us, and we had a wonderfully pleasant time. Mother was able to enjoy motor runs to Windsor and Kew and other places, and generally we finished up with tea at Bryanston Street, where John was living. I even saw a few plays.

It made all the difference to me having Maud to lean against, for we still had our bad times. All one night I went between Father with a heart attack in one room and Mother, delirious, in another.

But now we had the hope that the attacks would gradually decrease.

We were three months in London, and the inoculations were continued at home.

John had become prospective Unionist Candidate for the counties of Peebles and Selkirk. Loving the people and the countryside as he did, it was an ideal constituency for him, and he and Susie got a good deal of diversion and pleasure from their visits to supporters.

John had Harehope again that summer, and the parents were able to be there a good deal. It was a real summer, day after day of sunshine, so they were out nearly all the time. Naturally we were all greatly interested in John's political prospects and tried to help in any way we could. I became county secretary to the Women's Unionist Association and had to try to arouse interest in politics by getting up concerts and social meetings. How well we got to know every performer's *repertoire*! One elderly, rubicund Tory sang always the same two songs, always with great success—'The Lum-hat Wantin' the Croun,' and 'Jean Jameson's Bunnet.' He played his own accompaniment, and when he sang 'bunnet' he always gave a sort of double bounce on the piano-stool, which the audience waited for and found quite irresistible.

Sometimes I went with John to call on people, and found it very entertaining. Politics were seldom mentioned, but at one farm, where we had been most hospitably entertained, and hoped that we had made a good impression, the farmer came with us to the car, shook hands and said, " Well, good-bye. Thanks for your visit. I'll do all I can—against ye." John was amused, but I thought it was rather low behaviour. The sitting member, Sir Donald McLean, was a good member and very popular, so it did not seem probable that when an election came there would be any change, but J. B. was determined to do his utmost. He soon got to know most of the Unionists, and he would say as the chauffeur threaded his way down the narrow Old Town :

" Cautious, White. Whatever you do, don't kill a supporter."

A lot of John's friends came to speak for him, and everyone was delighted when F. E. Smith (as he was then) promised to come when he was in Scotland in September.

The Drill Hall was taken and all preparations made for a big gathering. But we ourselves were *very* uneasy. John, of course, had written to remind F. E. Smith of his promise, and also wired, but we knew that he and his wife were visiting about in the far north, and when we got no word we began to wonder if our reminder had reached him.

It came to the day of the meeting and no word had been received. That was a ' Sister-Anne-do-you-see-anybody-coming ' day. We watched the road winding over the moor like hawks, and car after car came on one errand or another, but—never the one we wanted. Six o'clock came. The meeting was at eight, and there would be barely time now for a rest and dinner, but still there was only the wind blowing and the grass growing. At six-thirty John, staring through glasses, shouted, " There's a car coming ! " As we watched it come up the winding road someone said in a tense voice, " If it's only people coming to call, we'll *kill* them."

Fortunately such extremes were not necessary, the car contained what we had hoped for, and the meeting was an enormous success. It was on the whole a very happy summer. 'Father and Mother both seemed stronger. They were able to drive about quite a lot, and just to be up on the moorland was sheer bliss to Father.

John and his family went back to London in October, and we settled down to the winter in Peebles, hoping and believing that it would be better than the last.

But in the end of October Mother took the worst attack she had had for months, and when she was slowly struggling up from it Father died.

He had been in bed for a few days with a slight chill, but was better. I was sitting with him, talking about cheerful things like Willie's next leave and Alastair's half-term holiday. I had turned away to do something to the fire, when, hearing a sound, I ran to the bed—to find him gone.

We, knowing what his life had been, thought that the summons had come for him, as for Mr. Standfast, " that his Master was not willing that he should be so far from Him any longer." And for him, as for Mr. Standfast, the river was low, he went over ' well nigh dry-shod.'

CHAPTER IX

"When I last rade down Ettrick,
The winds were shifting, the storm was waking,
The snow was drifting, my heart was breaking,
For we never again were to ride thegither
In sun or storm on the mountain heather;
When I last rade down Ettrick."

LADY JOHN SCOTT.

MY father's death seemed to remove part of the roof
of life, but there were various things that helped
us through the winter of 1911. Thankfulness that Mother
was, so far, well. We walked delicately for long, but as
the fever kept away we gained confidence and began to
hope that it had gone for good. John's first boy was born
the week Father died. As one John Buchan went out of
the world another came in, and the thought of the child
helped Mother. Then Willie's 'long leave' was due the
next summer, so the winter passed, and in April we planned
a holiday to Stratford-on-Avon. We had never attended
the Shakespeare Festival—though we adored him hardly
on this side of idolatry—and Warwickshire, indeed the
whole English country, was practically unknown to us.

We had acquired a car and meant to motor all the way,
stopping when and where the fancy took us; and we set
off one morning with the sun shining and Spring putting
a spirit of youth into everything—Mother, Walter, Maud,
Mark, and myself.

There is surely no more lovely road than the one we
took from Peebles to England, winding as it does by the
Tweed, past ancient Stobo Kirk, past lovely Dawyck,
past Drummelzier where Merlin sang his wild songs in
the dawning of the world, up to Linkumdoddie, the scene
of Burns' poem on Willie Wastle:

128

WILLIAM BUCHAN,

" Her face wad fyle the Logan Water—
Sic a wife as Willie had."

Next comes Crook and Tweedsmuir and the Source of
Tweed, then over the moors to the Devil's Beef Tub, that
great pit among the green hills of Annandale which, when
the mist swirls in it, seems to smoke like a cauldron, and
down into the sunny, quiet town of Moffat.

About Drummelzier we became aware that all was not
right with the car ; we seemed to go haltingly like a bird
with a broken wing. The chauffeur got out and had a
look at it, the rest of us, knowing about as much of the
working of cars as new-born babes, watching him anxiously.
We started again, only to stop after a few miles. What
made it so humiliating was that a wagonette from Broughton, driven by old William Newbigging whom we had
known from infancy, was going the same way. As we sat
on the roadside while the chauffeur tinkered with the
works, he passed us, flourishing his whip and grinning
broadly and (we suspected) derisively. This happened
four times, and we had no spirit left to resent the grin.
It looked as if the first part of our journey was going to be
a dismal failure. But at Moffat (where we lunched on
broth and fresh-caught salmon) the car was put to rights—
it had only been a small thing—and never again wavered.

The first night we spent in the Lake District, waking to
another perfect morning ; the next night we lay at Shrews-
bury, then through leafy Warwick lanes we arrived at
Stratford, the kingcups glistening in the meadows, the
hawthorn making snow in summer. We stayed at the
Shakespeare Hotel which then was Sir Frank Benson's
headquarters ; he and his wife had rooms in the genuinely
old part. To me it seemed a wonderful thing to be under
the same roof as a real live actor, to see him go in and out,
to hear him talk, and sometimes coach, in the generally

empty drawing-room, some young member of his company.

Naming the rooms after plays has its funny side. To see the most respectable boots of the Mayor and Mayoress of somewhere standing outside a door labelled *Anthony and Cleopatra* made one giggle. Mother's room was, most inappropriately, *Two Gentlemen of Verona*.

We stayed a week, and went every night and often in the afternoon to the theatre. At least Walter and I did; Mother was easily glutted with Shakespeare. Unlike Lord Lilac,

> " Who thought it rather rotten
> That Shakespeare should be quite forgotten,"

she was careless as to whether or not he was remembered. Not that she had any ill-will to him; but, as she told an American worshipper, she had never heard much to his credit.

" Oh, don't say," said the worshipper. " He had a great white soul."

But though she found the plays wearisome, she enjoyed Stratford. It had the kind of shops that appealed to her, full of things that she could buy to take home. She had a passion for little stucco figures of saints, and her mantel-shelf at home was crowded with them. Their heads were constantly being knocked off by careless dusting, and it was Alastair's task to stick them on. " I hope you don't mind," he said one day, " but Moses' head won't stay on unless I turn it round, so his beard's down his back."

In one Stratford shop, a mixed-up shop of cakes and crucifixes and little figures, presided over by a dignified lady with black lace on her head, Mother picked up a figure remarking that it would be a nice remembrance of Stratford.

" Oh, surely not, Madam," said the shocked voice of

the shop-lady, " surely a nobler memory," and when she
looked it was a figure of Christ. My poor mother fled,
dismayed, without paying, and I had to go back to explain.

I have seldom enjoyed anything more than that first
visit to Stratford. Not only the plays, but the lovely
surroundings, the drives to Warwick and Kenilworth, to
Broadway, and many enchanting, unspoiled Cotswold
villages. Since then we have paid many visits to Shakespeare's own town. In 1915, after visiting Alastair, who
was stationed at Sutton Verney before going to France,
we stood outside the Shakespeare Hotel and read *The
Times* poster about the first German gas attack.

We went back in 1919, when Giles Playfair produced
As You Like It, himself playing Touchstone. Athene
Seyler made a delicious Rosalind, and persuaded one,
against one's own judgment, that the lady ' more than
common tall ' looked exactly as she did.

Herbert Marshall was (I think) Jaques. There was a
note on the programme that the wrestling match was
rather a pretence, as the wrestlers had not long returned
from a more serious combat. We have seen many changes
in Stratford : a new theatre, new actors, the town filled
with Air Force men in a World War, but there has always
been the same delight at finding oneself in the old place,
and the same pang when we had to leave it.

Before leaving for our holiday I had finished my book
about India, and John read it and thought perhaps it might
find a publisher. I urged him to try Messrs. Hodder and
Stoughton, and it was accepted by that firm. My chief
pleasure in it was the thought of telling Willie.

It was July 1912 before he got his leave. He came home
rather tired, having had much extra work owing to the
partition of Bengal and other things, but in great spirits.

He had a lot to tell us about an eighteen days' leave that he and two friends had spent in Sikhim some time before. He wrote an article about it, which appeared in *Blackwood's Magazine*, along with a story by John. Mr. William Blackwood wrote:

" I read your article with intense interest and admiration, being struck by the power possessed by two brothers of such vivid descriptive writing."

It was a strenuous journey over ground never covered before by a European. They found the new route they were looking for, but they did not recommend it to future travellers.

This appreciation of the coolies was typical of Willie: " Here a word must be said in praise of the coolies. They were splendid fellows, and throughout the trek never gave a moment's trouble. Their cheerfulness was amazing. Each carried a load of sixty pounds. They swung downhill singing and whistling, uphill they groaned Ram Ram in mock distress. The camp arrangements were never delayed by a laggard coolie ; at night their brushwood fires were cheerful with laughter and music. The perpetual mist and rain never damped their spirits. Nights spent in wet clothes under flimsy leaking shelters they took as a matter of course ; in the morning they rolled out, smiling and cheerful as ever, to take up their packs made heavier by the rain. Throughout the episode of the jungle-cutting they never grumbled, and I can imagine no greater trial of temper than to carry a load through thick undergrowth. They were walking steadily for ten hours up and down many thousand feet of very trying country. It was an inspiration from Heaven that made them play at being a flock of sheep. The head-coolie played the shepherd, uttering weird, seductive calls, and the rest baa-ed in chorus. Mercifully the childish jest never grew stale.

The steeper the ground, the louder and more pathetic sounded the bleating. At the end of the day, when the shepherd limped into camp ahead of his flock, half-dead with exhaustion, he informed us gravely that the *bheri-walla* was very tired, and he had lost all his sheep."

Here is his description of the view from the Alukthana glacier :

" I have seen Kangchenjunga by moonlight from Darjeeling, and have thought it the *nunc dimittis* of scenery. The gossamer mist in the valleys like finest wood-smoke, lit as by softest invisible lamps, the labyrinth of ridges dimly distinct, yet softly fused in a silver light, melting upwards to a crown of purest white snow—it seemed that nothing could be more beautiful. But I had not then seen that vision from below the Alukthana glacier, when the mists slowly unveiled the face of Pandim to the moon. The solid rock buttresses of Kabru were sharply outlined in deepest black shadow ; shimmering mist shut off the valley to north and south ; only this delicate thing of white magic hovered above us. The words white and black convey no impression of the colours of the snow and rocks, nor can any words impoverished by common use. Her graceful lines were a luminous whiteness shining by a light of her own, and her cliffs conveyed an unearthly impression of transparency. It was like a vision from another world. Till far into the night three shivering mortals kept reverent vigil among the icy stones of the Praig Chu."

I was in London meeting Willie, and John and Susie made a great festival of his homecoming. The children, Alice and baby John, were at Peebles, otherwise there would hardly have been room in the little Bryanston Street house, more especially as Willie had such masses of luggage, and made such hay of the contents, without Pagett to lay things out for him.

We had a riotous week together. He was so good about always wanting me to do things with him. I must go with him to the tailor's to choose new clothes, and if I looked at a picture-paper while the choice was being made, "You're not taking an interest, Nan," he would say, and I had to give my mind seriously to the choice of patterns. It was a delight to go to the play, or to a party, with him, he enjoyed everything so whole-heartedly : the way he threw back his head and laughed would have encouraged the dullest to wit.

The weather was very hot that July in London—hotter than Calcutta, Willie thought. Then one day it changed suddenly, in the dangerous way our weather does, and became very cold. I thought Willie had got a chill and fussed a bit, but he laughed at me, and certainly he seemed in the best of spirits on our journey north. Perhaps he rather dreaded going home, fearing that the sight of him would bring back to Mother all that had happened since last they met, and hers was rather a tearful welcome, but the children were there to make things easier, and Alastair (Uncle As, as the children called him) grown up since last he had seen him, grinned bashfully in the background.

John and Susie came up in the beginning of August to Broadmeadows Cottage, Yarrow. It was only about twenty miles from Peebles, a lovely road.

For months we had been planning what we would do in Willie's 'long leave.' We hugged the thought that this time he would not leave us in autumn, this time we would keep him all through the winter, and through most of the spring and summer. Perhaps it was the winter time we thought of most. We thought of him coming back in the twilight from a long day in the open, coming down the

Old Town with its cheerful little lighted windows, into our old house, where there would be blazing fires and a hot bath and, after dinner, cosy times talking and laughing together. And John said he pictured himself coming home in the evening from the office to find Willie writing in the library, and how he would look up with the lift of the head that was so characteristic, and they would tell each other all the day's news before they went with Susie to the nursery to play with the babies ; and we hoped to go to Switzerland for winter sports—there was no end to the things we planned.

We dreamed dreams that were not to come true. Instead of the draught of joy we expected we had to drink the wine of astonishment.

Whether he had got some poison in his sytem which had lain dormant until he came back to our uncertain climate, we shall never know. Shortly after he came home he told me he had a queer kind of pain in his back which came every night at the same time. We persuaded him to see a doctor, who could find nothing and had him X-rayed. That showed nothing, and the doctors decided it was some form of rheumatism. He laughed about it himself, called it his mysterious Oriental pain, and he fished and shot and seemed quite happy, but we were uneasy.

Baths and massage at the Hydropathic did no good, the pain came and went just the same. In September some friends asked him to go with their party to the Oban Gathering, and we persuaded ourselves that he would be the better of the balls and all the fun. But when he came back we found that he had evidently not enjoyed it at all, and the pain was worse.

Then he took pleurisy, and the doctors advised us to take him to Glasgow to a nursing-home, where he would be near the specialist who was treating him.

The amazing thing was that he made those weeks in the Home almost pleasant to look back on. Our anxiety, of course, was terrible and unceasing, but in his room we had to put everything away except how to make things easier for him. When we thought what it meant to him— this was his 'long leave' that he had dreamed about for years, that he had expected to fill so full of work and play —his courage and gaiety were something to marvel at. Whatever his thoughts—and one does not lie in pain for weeks without long thoughts—he kept them from us.

Propped up in bed, looking so boyish, and so oddly well with his flushed face and eager blue eyes, he would stick his monocle in his eye, and, addressing Alastair as 'Stout fellow,' chaff him about his Fabian Society. He insisted on knowing exactly what Mother had eaten for luncheon, and worried if he thought I hadn't an interesting book—this in the midst of great and constant pain. And seeing him so brave for very shame's sake we were brave too. We saved up every little funny thing we saw or heard to tell him, and he never failed to look interested, and laugh.

John could not rest away from him, and spent his time rushing between London and Glasgow.

When the proof-sheets of my book *Olivia in India* arrived from the publishers, Willie read them through in one day, almost forgetting where he was in his interest in reading the account of what we had done together. When he had finished it he said, " I don't know what the reading public will think of it, but for a whole day it has made me forget my miserable self."

He died on November 11th, 1912.

There was one ray of comfort in the aching darkness of our grief, he had died at home.

As J. B. wrote in his " W. H. B. *Fratri Dilectissimo*," the dedication to *Montrose* :

"One boon the Fates relenting gave—
   Not where the scented hill-wind blows
From cedar thickets lies your grave,
   Nor mid the steep Himálayan snows.
Night calls the stragglers to the nest,
   And at long last 'tis home indeed
For your far-wandering feet to rest
   Forever by the crooks of Tweed."

When the news of his death reached India, the *Statesman* wrote :

"The influence of Mr. Buchan's work on behalf of the debt-ridden cultivator of the soil will be felt long after his fellow civilians have left India. His work was thorough, his friendship was warm, and his sympathies wide. The loss of his personality will be felt not only in the circle of his intimate friends, but in every village in the Province where his visits were looked forward to by the people he tried to help. Bengal can ill afford to lose officers of the stamp of William Buchan."

"He did his work from higher motives than most of us," one man who worked with him wrote, and another :

"There was about him an atmosphere more clean, more straight, more brave than I met with elsewhere. He was in every way a type dear to the imagination but so seldom met with in the flesh that the loss is doubly hard to bear. Of all the men I know he was the one I would have gone to in any deep trouble or distress of mind and body."

And poor 'Pagett,' in the most pathetic letter I ever read, said, "Further I beg to pray there will not be found in the world such a master as my master was."

CHAPTER X

(Behind the walls at Arras)
" *Who are those men who rush on death ?* "
CYRANO DE BERGERAC.

NOTHING seemed to matter much that winter, but we got through it. Mother and I felt we had to keep up for Alastair's sake. When he came into a room where we were he always gave a quick glance at our faces, and if he saw we had been crying, went quietly out again. But, fortunately, he was kept hard at work in his classes at Glasgow University, and in the holidays we saw to it that he had always friends staying.

In the early spring of 1913 I was in London with John and Susie. They had left Bryanston Street and gone to Portland Place, to a delightful, spacious house with beautifully proportioned rooms, and John was interested in finding just the right pieces of furniture for each room : he was always very house proud.

While I was there my book *Olivia in India* slipped unobtrusively into the world. I remember with gratitude how kind people were about it, not only my own people but many others, and especially I remember the encouragement given me by Susie's mother, Mrs. Norman Grosvenor, herself a writer of great ability, and Mrs. Belloc-Lowndes. I did not want to use my name as (in my opinion) John had given lustre to the name of Buchan which any literary efforts of mine would not be likely to add to, so I called myself ' O. Douglas.' It did not strike me at the time that it was rather a daring thing to publish a book in which practically all the incidents were true and in which the characters could all recognise themselves and each other ; in some cases the names were not even altered. In the most ostrich-like way I thought that by not putting my own name on the title-page I had made everything all right.

One never knows what will upset people. One man was hurt in his feelings because I revealed that he sang hymns on Sunday night, and two worthy ladies were never the same to me after I described them as good but dowdy.

It was an immense surprise to me to find my book well reviewed by many reputable papers, and James Douglas in the *Star* gave it a whole column, remarking that when one found a happy book everyone should be told about it.

John's advice to me was, " Never worry your publisher, and don't let what critics say worry you."

He was right about the publisher, but I have always been inclined to treat critics with great respect and been most grateful to them for a kind word. It would be a pity, though, to worry about a slighting review, for, after all, critics are but mortal men. There may be a reason for a critic's treatment of a book or a play which has nothing to do with its merits or demerits. He may have had a bad dinner or quarrelled with his wife, or feel that he is taking influenza and be in a mood to ban and not to bless. Or an old-fashioned critic (if any such exist) gets hold of a book by iconoclastic youth and promptly rends it. A modern, suspicious of sentiment, hot for the bitter burning stuff of life, picks up a pretty, gentle story of happy, fortunate people, and, naturally, stamps on it.

And there is always the consolation of remembering that when critics themselves write a book or a play it is not always the masterpiece one would expect.

Anyway *Olivia* got better reviews than it deserved and has gone into many editions.

In July of that summer (1913) we went for a cruise,

J. B. and Susie, Mother, Walter, and I. Some people are good at going cruises, others are not, and we belong to the latter class. The ship was the one I went to India on (it was sunk by a submarine in 1917) and smelt just as cockroachy as it did then. There were crowds of people on board and the fun was fast and furious. A gang of noisy young girls (whom we christened 'Nymphs surprised while bathing'), ably abetted by a gang of youths, kept things going to their own great satisfaction.

One reason why we did not enjoy the cruise was that J. B. was seedy most of the time. He was beginning to have the gastric trouble that pursued him all his life and the food did not suit him. Susie had a cough (named Albert), and I was seasick given the slightest provocation. Walter played games, made friends, and was quite happy. Mother occupied herself by writing her life in pencil in a tuppeny notebook and reading it aloud to me as I lay seasick in my bunk.

The days on shore were quite pleasant. We went to Madeira and Gibraltar, where John found some fine Chinese cabinets for the Portland Place drawing-room, and admired the hedges of pink geraniums at Algeciras. Our visit to Lisbon was made memorable by the fact that someone threw a bomb while we were there, and we engaged a taxi-man who did not seem to know his right hand from his left, who had no brakes, and who yelled at the top of his voice all the time, inciting other taxi-men to race him. At the Azores we went an expedition on ponies and saw some lovely scenery. At Santiago we had an uneasy luncheon, as the band at short intervals insisted on playing the British national anthem, which meant that most of the time we were on our feet.

There were a lot of most interesting people on board whose acquaintance we only made the last day or two. It served us right for peevishly keeping ourselves to ourselves.

1914 began well with a beautiful spring. We went to Stratford Festival in April, where we were joined by Walter and his friend Robbie MacMillan, with whom he had been having a walking tour in Belgium. Robbie was then minister of St. John's, Kensington, a brilliant young preacher and philosopher. When the war came he joined up as a combatant and was killed at Arras in 1917.

In July I was in Devonshire with G. my old ship-mate, staying with her sister. Mrs. Turner and her husband were now home from Calcutta and settled in a charming house near Sidmouth. Devonshire was new to us both and we spent long pleasant days raking round the countryside, exploring Exeter, visiting countless delicious little villages, wandering on the moors, and talking continually.

G. was amused at my new interest in politics. The Irish Question was then very much in the foreground, that smouldering fire of hate and distrust which faded into insignificance before the great conflagration of the First German War, but, unhappily, is still smouldering. We had been visited in Peeblesshire by Ulster men who had come over to do propaganda work, and one of them told me about a visit he had paid to one of the local clergy. " ' We'll have a word of prayer about it,' he says, but he hadn't been speaking for two minutes when I knew it was a Home Rule God he was praying to."

In the end of July, as I left Euston for Scotland, I saw *John Bull's* poster, " To Hell with Servia."

The first weeks of August were a strange time. The banks were closed for the moratorium and we were inundated by acquaintances who had been caught touring in their cars and wanted some money to get home. We read newspapers until we were dazed, and began furiously to knit. Belgian strongholds were falling one by one. "Uhlans" was the terrifying word that we whispered to each other. One thought of them as fabulous monsters, like the giants of our childhood, till one day I noticed in the papers that the Germans marching in the heat were suffering from their feet. That seemed to change everything; they ceased to be monsters and became men like other men, tired and footsore, wondering, perhaps, why they had to fight.

Shortly we got to work—canteens, sewing-meetings, serving men's wives to look after—and our lives fell into the new design.

Walter found that his job would be to stay at home and do the dull jobs—not an easy task for a man of military age. Alastair took his degree in October and went off at once to train with the O.T.C. somewhere in England. "Only for home service," Mother begged. Hers was the old cry. "*Simeon is not, Joseph is not, wilt thou take Benjamin also?*" But this Benjamin was so willing to go.

As the war started J. B. had the ill fortune to be sent to bed for six weeks with a duodenal ulcer. To make the time pass during those six weeks he wrote his story *The Thirty-Nine Steps*, the first of the Richard Hannay books. It came out in *Blackwood's Magazine* anonymously, and there was much speculation about the author. Up to that time J. B. had written some half-dozen novels : *John Burnet of Barns*, *The Half-hearted*, *A Lost Lady of Old Years*, *Prester John*, and, in 1912, a collection of short stories called *The Moon Endureth*. It was highly praised, and I remember how pleased he was when "Q" wrote to him saying he would have been proud to have written the one called *The Lemnian*.

Though his novels sold fairly well he was not what one would call a popular novelist, but with *The Thirty-Nine Steps*, followed by *Greenmantle* and all the other Hannay books, he became a best-seller. Those books were a great deal more than mere thrillers. They struck a note of poetry and high courage which set them above other contemporary work in that field.

Only the other day someone writing in the *Scotsman* deplored the absence in this war of such stories of adventure, and was replied to by a devoted student of Buchaniana (a young soldier) who pointed out the sobering fact that even if John Buchan had still been alive his familiar and well-loved little band of characters would have been getting no younger. He proceeded to give the age today of each character—Richard Hannay 66, and so on, but none of them too old to help. Richard Hannay, he fancied, would have spent the first nine months of the war badgering the Secretary for War for a job, and would then have found a niche as a Home Guard Zone Commander. Clanroyden would somehow or other have got out to the Middle East where his ability to pass as an Arab would come in handy, while Lamancha would have adorned the War Cabinet. John Scantlebury Blenkiron would have been a moving spirit in Lease Lend on the other side of the Atlantic ; and on one point he was wholly convinced, Mr. Dickson McCunn would have dipped deep in his capacious pocket and would have subscribed for a whole Squadron of Spitfires for the R.A.F. In August (1943), while Susie was staying with us in Peebles, this same young soldier gave a broadcast on the characters of the Richard Hannay books, and as we listened we felt not only touched but comforted that they should, after twenty years, be so much alive.

One can realise that it must have been a great pleasure to J. B. to write those books. Into them he put all his longing for action and adventure that his health would not allow him to experience. Although he worked very hard he was never well at that time, and when in 1916 he was sent out to G.H.Q. as a liaison officer, he must have had a pretty bad time. Rocketing about in a car in awful weather over awful roads from one part of the line to another, seldom out of pain, to take his mind off himself he composed poems about the Scottish fighting-men in France. One, *On Leave*, describes a man going home on leave in time to bury his child, and who wanders on the Lammerlaw with :

> " The stink o' the gas in my nose,
>   The colour o' bluid in my e'e,
> And the bidding o' Hell in my lug
>   To curse my Maker and dee."

At first utterly despairing, gradually the familiar sounds, the murmur of the burns, the kindly vision of sheep, the cry of the whaup, and the sweet smells of a summer evening on a quiet hillside, brought him to his senses, and he was able to say :

> " Loos and the Lammerlaw,
>   The battle was fought in baith.
> Death was round and abune,
>   But life in the heart of death.
> A' the world was a grave,
>   But the grass on the graves was green,
> And the stanes were bields for hames,
>   And the laddies played atween.
> Kneelin' aside the cairn,
>   On the heather and thymy sod,
> The place I had kenned as a bairn,
>   I made my peace with God."

J. B. always said he was no poet, merely a bard, but he could speak to the heart of his countrymen.

In the early spring of 1917 he was made Minister of Information under the Prime Minister, but the doctors insisted that before he began the work there must be an operation. It was done at his home in Portland Place, and when he was getting over it I was allowed to be with him. He had two splendid nurses, Nurse Raw from Aberdeen, and Nurse Tabeteau, who had a voice like a bird. In spite of everything that convalesence was a happy time. Susie was so relieved to have him at home, to see him out of pain and able to enjoy food. He was a good patient, perfectly contented to lie in bed and to read and read and talk and laugh, till he could begin work again. When he was able, he and Susie and I went to Checkendon, the F. S. Olivers' place in Buckinghamshire, kindly lent to John. Dougal Malcolm and his wife were there too, and it was fine to walk in the beechwoods in the spring sunshine, and in the evenings to hear such good talk round the fire. It was like a spell of halcyon weather among raging storms. John had only been back at work a few days when he got the news that his little brother, and his partner and great friend, Tommy Nelson, had been killed in the Battle of Arras.

Looking back we could see that Alastair had been born for the Great War. He had an extraordinarily interesting life as a boy. It was as if we had been allowed to give him every single pleasure that we could, that we might be glad afterwards. He never seemed to take much interest in his own future, but to live in the present, always contented and gay. When he finished at Glasgow University it was arranged he should go into Mr. Maxtone Graham's office in Edinburgh to get some knowledge of business. He began in June 1914, and we have a notebook in which he made his first attempts at book-keeping : *Alastair Buchan in account with self.* It is an account much ornamented by funny faces (for he was a fair caricaturist), and not very accurate, for sums are frequently noted as ' lost.' It stops suddenly, and underneath the last entry is scrawled, " *The War here intervened.*"

He joined the Cameron Highlanders with many men of his year, and was sent to Aldershot, and then to Bramshott. Things were still in a state of chaos ; food was bad and insufficient, the huts leaked, the mud was awful, but he had no complaints. He did not even grumble at his uniform, which consisted of a red tunic (made in 1880 for a man of six feet and broad in proportion) and a pair of exceedingly bad blue trousers. This was his job, this was what he had been waiting for, and he went into it with his whole heart. Writing in the beginning of 1917 he said, " These last two years have been the happiest of my life."

He first went to France in 1915, with the 9th Battalion of the Royal Scots Fusiliers. For a time Mr. Winston Churchill was their Colonel, and was extremely popular. He was particularly kind to the young officers, and on at least one occasion managed to get horses for them, and they rode in to dinner at the nearest town. Alastair liked to tell us how he said, " War is a game to be played with a smile, and if you can't manage to smile, with a grin."

Later Mr. Winston Churchill wrote of him : " He was a very charming and gallant young officer, and much liked by his comrades. I knew him well enough to understand how great his loss must be to those who knew him better, and to those who knew him best of all."

Alastair was wounded in February 1916, and was kept at Rosyth training men all the summer. It was great luck for us, for he got out to Broughton fairly often for weekends, and now and again for some leave. In October he returned to France. His letters were like himself, kind and happy. He wrote in the train going up the line :

" . . . Last night I made a composite meal in the train, chocolates, sardines, canned peaches, and tea—eaten in that order. Then I fell asleep, and, probably as a result of the sardines, I had a queer dream. I thought I was a small boy again, and I couldn't find you. I woke up shouting, ' Mother ! ' to the delight of the other men in the carriage. Don't worry, and keep well. I am so jolly myself and it makes me feel selfish if I think you are worrying."

One could see from his letters how much he liked his men and his fellow-officers.

" There's a decent lad in my platoon who heard me say my dug-out was draughty, and he went away and filled up all the chinks with sandbags, and made a shutter for the window. Now it's a grand frowst ! "

Later : " There are two corporals in my company that I love. They are both wonderful and don't know what fear is—a thing that a timid man like myself marvels at. Also they have an uncanny sense of direction, and are kindly disposed to their weaker brother (that's me again). They form my bodyguard, and every time I fall into a shell-hole or dodge a crump you can hear them shout, ' Are ye hurt, sirr ? '

" . . . Shiel wakened us this morning by rushing into the dug-out shouting, ' Get up ! The Huns are only 100 yards off ! ' which, though it sounds startling, was true. Shiel is the kindest-hearted and most conscientious man I ever struck. Although he loathes the whole business, and is older than the rest of us, he never grouses. Last night I asked him to waken me at 11 so that I could go out and see my wiring-party. He didn't waken me but went out himself, so that I got two hours' extra sleep.

" . . . I spent Christmas taking a working-party up the line. We got shelled and sniped and met the Brigadier— I don't know which was the worst. I am writing this in a perfect Babel of noise. In the tent are Shiel, Browning,

Cooper (a regular) and myself. (Browning writes poetry and incessantly argues on art ; he also speaks in his sleep. Last night I was wakened by him muttering, ' And the horrible thing about it is that, artistically, the only thing that pleases me is Hun music ! ')   At present we are having a great argument about Stonewall Jackson.   Browning is considering him from a ' literary ' standpoint.   Cooper is telling us what he learned about him at Sandhurst, while Shiel is reciting *Barbara Frietchie*."

Sometimes he would admit that they had had a trying forty-eight hours in the front trenches, up to the waist in liquid mud, and no food but a dry biscuit ; but he always finished, " One can stand anything for forty-eight hours."

We sent him every single thing we could think of.   He loved all eatables, but books were his chief stay.   Susie sent him Chesterton's Poems, which were a delight to him, and almost the last things he read were Gilbert Murray's *Hippolytus* and *The Bacchae*, sent him by the children.

His leave was due in March, and he longed eagerly for home, but when the battalion was moved to Arras he knew, as he put it, that his leave had gone very far west.

On the morning of April 10th we read in the papers that a great battle had begun at Arras, and that same morning a letter came from Alastair that was almost like a good-bye.

" My dearest Motherkin,

" Yesterday was the Sabbath.   There was no Presbyterian, so I attended a C.E. service, which was nice and quiet and simple.   We read a most appropriate psalm about the terror by night, etc.   We expect to move tomorrow and there may be a stoppage of letters for a few days, but don't worry, wee body.

" We've had a fine rest this last week, and I've enjoyed every minute of it.   I shall be in command of the company for a short time now. Old Shiel is getting a rest which he has certainly earned.

" There may be things happening, but don't worry about me. I was just thinking last night what a good time I've had all round and what a lot of happiness. Even the sad parts aren't sad any longer, but, in a queer way, a comfort. . . ."

His last letter, which came three days after he fell, was written just before the attack :

" . . . I got a splendid mail last night. Letters from J. B. and you and Walter and Nana, and a Fuller's cake, and *The Sketch* and *Tatler*. John wrote me a *very* kind letter. I shall answer it as soon as poss. We are very comfortable here ; the only thing is we are short of cigarettes. Old Shiel and I bade each other a tearful farewell last night. He is one of the best men that ever was.

" I do hope you are well and cheerful.

" Very much love from your very aff. son,

" ALASTAIR."

At dawn on April 9th (Easter Monday) he led his company in the attack. They were in the German second line when he was hit heavily by shrapnel. At the aid-post he was so cheerful that the Colonel wrote to us that he was only slightly wounded and would soon be home.

Alastair once wrote of his Colonel : " It's a pleasure to work for Col. Gordon. He has been awfully kind to me, and I'd hate to disappoint him."

He did not disappoint him. Colonel Gordon wrote of him :

" I told you I promoted him specially over the heads of others, not because he was John Buchan's brother, but because he was Alastair Buchan, a most excellent fellow. During the bombardment before the battle he had occasion to send me reports and ask questions about equipment, etc., and various preparations in connection with the attack, and in every case I thought to myself as I read these reports and answered the questions, 'Now that really is a thoroughly reliable officer.' . . . I shall always remember him as I saw him last, about 4.45 a.m. on April 9th as I left my dug-out to go round his company for the last time: I shook hands with him and wished him good luck." . . .

John was at G.H.Q. the week after, and a 'Fusilier Jock' took him to the grave. He visited the field-hospital and spoke to the sister-in-charge, who very kindly wrote to us. She said that Alastair and another boy, Gervase Maude, were brought in together. Nothing could be done for them, and they died in a few minutes. When she had washed the battle-grime from their faces and smoothed their flaxen hair, they looked mere children, and, knowing that somewhere over the Channel hearts would break for these bright heads, before they were laid in the earth she kissed them for their mothers.

The following verses were written by J. B. in 1917 for a privately printed booklet, *Alastair Buchan* :

> "Long, long ago, when all the lands
>   Were deep in peace as summer sea,
>   God chose his squires and trained their hands
>   For those stern lists of liberty.
>
> You made no careful plans for life,
>   Happy with dreams and books and friends,
>   Incurious of our worldly strife,
>   As dedicate to nobler ends. . . .
>
> I mind how on the hills of home
>   You ever lagged and strayed aside,
>   A brooding boy whose thoughts would roam
>   O'er gallant fates that might betide.

But not the wildest dreams of youth,
Born of the sunset and the spring,
Could match the splendour of the truth
That waited on your journeying—

The ancient city deep in night,
The wind among its crumbling spires,
The assembly in the chill twilight,
Murky with ghosts of wayward fires;

The last brave words,[1] the outward march,
The punctual shells, whose ceaseless beat
Made the dark sky an echoing arch
Pounded without by demon feet;

While with the morn wild April blew
Her snows across the tortured mead,
The spring-time gales that once you knew
In glens beside the founts of Tweed;

And then the appointed hour; the dread
Gun-flare that turned the sleet to flame,
When, the long vigil o'er, you led
Your men to purge the world of shame.

You did not fall till you had won
The utmost trench and knew the pride
Of a high duty nobly done
And a great longing satisfied.

You left the line with jest and smile
And heart that would not bow to pain—
I'll lay me down and bleed awhile,
And then I'll rise and fight again.

.   .   .   .   .   .

I stood beside your new-made grave,
And as I mused my sorrow fled,
Save for those mortal thoughts that crave
For sight of those whom men call dead.

---

[1] We were told in a letter that as they waited for zero hour Alastair spoke ' words of comfort and encouragement ' to his men.

I knew you moved in ampler powers,
A warrior in a purer strife,
Walking that world that shall be ours
When death has called us dead to life.

The rough white cross above your breast,
The earth ungraced by flower or stone,
Are bivouac marks of those that rest
One instant ere they hasten on.

More fit such graves, than funeral pile,
Than requiem dirge the ballad strain:
I'll lay me down and bleed awhile,
And then I'll rise and fight again."

CHAPTER XI

"How wilt thou do in the swelling of Jordan?"

THE war went wearily on, with ever-increasing casualty
lists until it seemed as if we were to have no friends
left. Sometimes one looked round and was aware of a
great emptiness. I remember John saying that our world
was like the stalls at an unpopular play, one here, another
yonder, and wide gaps between.

Fortunately there was always work to do, and I found
my greatest comfort in my visits to homes in connection
with the Soldiers' and Sailors' Families Association.

My district was the Northgate and Cuddyside, and few
of my wives were at all well-off. They were most repaying
people to visit, and we got very intimate and laughed and
cried together. Their patience and courage shamed me
often, and their sense of humour rarely failed. And they
were all different, some had such tidy houses and 'genty'
ways; others frankly enjoyed a stir-about.

One woman, Mrs. Cassidy, with a surprising number of
small children, was a perpetual astonishment. Large and
good-natured, she seemed to spend her days leaning up
against a broom and gossiping with her neighbours, while
her room and kitchen seethed with her offspring. Seven,
I believe, was the actual number, but they were all so near
an age, so active and so omnipresent, that it was difficult
to count them or to know one from another.

The eldest, Danny-boy, took ill, and lay in a corner of
the dark kitchen, while the two youngest, who couldn't
walk, played on the top of him. One day the doctor told
Mrs. Cassidy that a children's specialist was coming out
the next day to see another case and he would bring him

153

in to see her boy. She told me this, very importantly, and I longed to suggest that she should tidy her house and herself in preparation for the visit, but I knew my place, and only hinted vaguely that specialists were, rather oddly perhaps, very particular about cleanliness and fresh air. Early the next morning when I went down to see if I could do anything to help, I found, to my horror, Mrs. Cassidy in a quite alarming state of undress, whitewashing the kitchen, while the sick boy, wrapped in a blanket, lay before the fire; the rest of the family being locked in the room.

"D'ye see me?" she said archly. "I'm just giving the place a dicht-up afore the specialist comes."

Whether it was the result of the specialist's visit or the whitewash I cannot say, but Danny-boy began to recover from that day.

One poor mother who had lost both her boys felt remiss that she had not died of grief.

She said, "And ma neebor there just lost the one, and *she* died, and folk said she never lifted her head after her laddie went, and here I am gaun aboot quite healthy."

I tried to tell her that, being strong, she had the harder part of going on with most of the joy of life wiped out, but I fear she still felt she had fallen short. It is pathetic how some of us in times of danger try to propitiate the Almighty. It was heart-breaking to hear a woman say, "I'll no' pray nae mair. I've prayed even on that Alick wad be spared, and yesterday, when it was sic an ill day, I brought in Mistress Gibson's three bairns—their mother was oot washin'—and gied them a hot meal and used up near all I had in the hoose, and they were hardly gone when the news came that Alick was deid."

When the war came I began to write a book in my few leisure moments. It was really written for my mother, an attempt to reconstruct for her our home-life in Glasgow. My father was in it; and Alastair (Buff, I called him), all his funny ways and sayings as far as I could remember them—I hoped he would read them himself and laugh— and most of the characters were composite portraits of people we had known. In describing the last days of an old Border woman I put in the remark of my friend in the tenement above the railway: "There's ma denner awa' by." In my usual ostrich-like way, I never thought of her seeing it, but the next time I paid her a visit, she fixed me with a stern eye, and said, "What for did ye mak me dee in a book?" It was supposed to begin in 1913, so the War came into it: the last chapters were written after Alastair had gone, and into them went some of my own grief.

Mother was sleeping badly at that time, and once when she was deploring the fact that no one seemed to write the kind of book she wanted to help her through the nights, I gave her the typescript to read.

This book, I felt, was too intimate, too home-made, to be published, but when J. B. read the MS., to my surprise he got quite excited about it (he was no lover of mild domestic fiction), and sent it off to Sir Ernest Hodder-Williams.

I had called the story 'Plain Folk,' but Sir Ernest said that was not an attractive title. Women, who are the chief novel readers, are not supposed to like plain folk. Some certainly don't—the lady in the Glasgow tram-car who was heard to say, "Jessie got a prize, *A Kiss for Cinderella*. Her Aunt Maggie reads a lot and she mentioned that the hero was a policeman. Imagine! I wrote to the headmistress! You would think, wouldn't you, that in an expensive school like that they would be more particular?"

The name chosen was *The Setons*, and the book was

dedicated to my mother in memory of her two sons, with the words :

> " They sought the glory of their country,
> they see the glory of God."

It came out in November 1917, and almost immediately a stream of letters began to pour in from all sorts of people. The one I liked best was from a man in the trenches. He wrote : " I'm a Glasgow man myself and it's pure Balm of Gilead to me."

Some wrote from distant parts of the Empire saying they could never hope to see the " blessed, beastly place " again, but now when the longing for it came over them, they could sit down with *The Setons* and smell the rain in the Glasgow streets.

So numerous were the letters that Walter advised me to have my replies typed, but that seemed a stiff mechanical way to answer friendly people, and I wrote in reply to everyone who wrote to me. Through these letters I made many friends in far places whom I shall never see, but who have written to me regularly for years, giving me news of their families and asking for news of mine. High up among my book-friends is Katharine Burrill, herself a writer. She wrote to me first because she recognised in *The Setons* so many things (like the singing of ' Prophet Daniel ') which belonged to her own Scots childhood. When we met we discovered we had many tastes in common, and from that day she has been a loyal and inspiring friend. Her letters are something to look forward to and remember, whether she is writing of books and plays, of people, or the world situation.

She was a friend of Ellen Terry, and once took me to see her. I never had the good fortune to see her act except in *Alice Sit-by-the-Fire*, but hers was a voice that once heard could not be forgotten. Once, when walking along the garden-side of Princes Street two ladies passed me. One with a cape and a mushroom hat and dark glasses, said to her companion, " There is an afternoon train from the Caledonian "—a prosaic utterance, but the voice was so beautiful that I stopped dead, then turned back to see the face that belonged to the voice—and recognised Ellen Terry.

When I was taken to see her she was in bed, old and ill and almost blind, but her voice was as lovely as ever, and when she questioned us about the play we had seen, and talked and laughed, we hung on her lips as thousands had done all her life.

Mine, of course, was a very small success, but a man who had written one of the biggest best-sellers of the day told me that nearly all the letters he got wanted something from him. My correspondents, on the other hand, seemed anxious to bestow things on me, and I have been greatly touched, and in these war-days, much benefited, by the thoughtful kindness of friends afar.

The letters and the new friends naturally brought much interest, not only to me but to Mother. Very often people wrote asking if they might come to see me. They came to see me, but they went away murmuring, " *What* a pleasure to meet your mother."

It was not surprising that Mother should steal the thunder. No one had such a welcoming way as she had. The shyest and most awkward visitor was at home with her at once. J. B., in *Memory Hold-the-Door*, talks of her tenderness for bores. But she simply did not recognise them as such. To her (unless they were snobs and climbers, and even of them she only said, " Poor souls ") everyone was of interest, and she had the art of getting the best out of everyone. Someone said that she warmed the atmosphere of the half of Scotland. Certainly everyone who came in contact with her felt her friendliness. Especially was she tender to lonely people. When I suggested that it was rather unusual to kiss someone she had met for the first time that afternoon, she said, " A lonely girl, working for her bread : was there any harm in it ? "

Among the multitude of letters that came when she died was one from this same girl. " I can never forget," she wrote, " that the one and only time that I met your mother she kissed me. It did much to encourage and help me over a rough bit of road."

So many say to me, " How *sweet* your mother was," and I smile acquiescently, but inwardly protest. She had far too acute a judgment to be what most people mean by ' sweet.' She had a wide tolerance. Like Falstaff she might have said, " Tush, man ; mortal men . . .", but on occasions she could be devastating in her criticism, though she preferred to hold her peace.

To her children she was a frank and fearless commentator. Love was not blind in her case, it made her the more clear-sighted. Because she was such an adoring mother she could not bear to see us fall below the standard she had set for us.

The works of her eldest son were naturally a great pride. Each one was sent to her with a suitable inscription, and was a treasured possession. The Lives of Scott and Montrose she read with delight, and she gazed with respect at Cromwell and Augustus, but it was a trial to her that she could make so little of his adventure stories. It made her feel slightly disloyal. She always kept the new one on her table, announcing that she was going to enjoy it when she could get a really undisturbed time. I am bound to say that when Mother did begin she gave the book every chance. Tea over and dinner still in the distance, she settled herself in her own particular chair, with a good light behind her and began. I liked to watch her face from where I sat writing. At first it was calm and interested, but after a few pages she would murmur, " Tuts, they're beginning to swear already." When I pointed out that it was true to life, these were rough fellows, she only shook her head. Presently, with a discouraged sigh, she would lay down the book, remarking, " Now he's got them into a cave and it's so confusing, I think I'll knit for a little." And then she sighed again at her own inability to appreciate her son's works. She sighed a great deal, my mother, and invariably looked on the dark side—but always with a twinkle in her eyes. Bishop Walpole, who was a great friend, said that her pessimism was like the bubbles on a glass of champagne.

But if J. B.'s books were beyond her, mine delighted her heart. They were as pure and almost as sweet as homemade toffee, their pages insullied by swear-words, and they were about happy comfortable people. Like Dr. John Brown's sister she might have said, " They are very nice people—so like ourselves."

My mother had never heard of inhibitions, and approved strongly of reticence, so it was as well that I had neither the will nor the ability to write a ' strong ' book. It amazes me what some writers put down on paper, and it is not that they do not get time for repentance, for they must see it in handwriting, in typescript, and in proofs.

A critic once complained of the lack of plot in my books, and I besought J. B. to think of one for me.

" Oh yes," he said brightly, " I'll give you a plot. Why don't you write about the Burke and Hare murders ? "

As if I had the sort of pen that could write about murders ! It is perhaps impertinent for a person with only a very small talent to try to write at all.

Thomas Hardy said, " A tale must be exceptional enough

to justify its telling. We tale-tellers are all Ancient Mariners, and no one of us is warranted in stopping wedding-guests (in other words, the hungry public) unless we have something more unusual to relate than the ordinary experiences of the average man or woman."

That shook me until I reminded myself that there are millions of people who would never dream of reading Thomas Hardy who get immense comfort and pleasure from a tale about the experiences of some average man and woman.

Kipling sang the song of such simple tale-tellers.

> " All's well—all's well aboard her—she's left you far behind,
>   With a scent of old-world roses through the fog that ties you blind.
>   Her crew are babes or madmen ? Her port is all to make ?
>   You're manned by Truth and Science, and you steam for steaming's sake ?
>   Well, tinker up your engines—you know your business best.
>   *She's* taking tired people to the Islands of the Blest ! "

In the war years people needed any comfort they could get, and yet, even against such a background of sadness and dread, one could at times be almost happy and carefree. There are pleasant things to remember, like summer months at Broughton with John's children—two were born in the war, Willie's namesake in 1915, and Alastair's in 1918.

It was very nice for me the way Susie shared the children with me ; I always paid them a visit in the spring, and treats were kept ' until Auntie Nan comes,' so that they learned to associate my coming with all sorts of pleasures. " Spring and Auntie Nan come together," they said.

It was always interesting to visit the Portland Place house—one met so many amusing people. One dinner-party I particularly remember, in 1916, which was given for a delegation of the Russian Duma visiting England. I sat beside Protopopov and found him quite delightful. He was so graceful, and quick and animated, and recited to me nursery rhymes, which, he said, he had learned from an English governess. " Alas ! " he said, " my English is nursery English." It was sad to hear that the Bolsheviks had shot him in prison.

In the spring of 1918 there were a good many air-raids on London. Four in one week I came in for. The children minded them not at all. When they were wakened, without a word they got up, put on their dressing-gowns and slippers and proceeded sedately to the basement where beds were ready for them in the wine-cellar. They hoped very much that I would be scared, and waited expectantly to hear me scream.

What a lot of different kinds of courage there are ! People who behave with the greatest fortitude when bombs are dropping may be utterly demoralised by the mere thought of a burglar creeping about the house ; others, who have been known to achieve feats of great daring, will make a prodigious fuss about a stiff neck.

The family did not come to Scotland in 1918, and Mother had such a quiet restful summer at Broughton that she began to feel that she was leading too idle a life. One night she said, " If we were here for the winter I would try to do something to make life more interesting for the women in the village, perhaps have them to this house one night a week. We would have tea and knit and sew, and sometimes get someone to talk to us about things in the world outside that we might learn something."

That same thought must have occurred to others, for shortly after that the Women's Rural Institutes came into being—a scheme that has revolutionised country life.

Now, practically every village in Scotland has its ' Rural,' and in practically every case it has proved a boon. I know of no pleasanter place to visit than a Women's Institute Meeting—and I have been to many in Scotland, England, and Canada—because of the spirit of friendliness and interest that pervades each one of them.

In the remote villages of our land the women had little to interest them outside their homes and families ; some of them, miles from a church or a shop, rarely saw a neighbour ; but the coming of the 'Rural' changed all that. Now they have a meeting of their own (in many cases held in a hall built by their own endeavour) where they can hear talks on all sorts of subjects, learn to make things, to join in competitions, and act in plays. They have even a magazine, ably edited, of their own.

The Drama Festival has discovered much unsuspected talent. A W.R.I. team with someone capable to coach them can make a wonderful show. I saw one from a Border village do a very simple human sketch about an old woman, too frail to keep her own little place any longer, preparing to go sadly to a Home. The scene was a cottage kitchen. The old wag-at-the-wa', the china dogs with painted gilt chains, the dresser with its brightly coloured bowls, were all there. The kindly neighbours, the efficient nurse, having said their say, went out and the old woman is left nursing the 'bonnie blue jug' that her man had bought her in Kelso when they were first married. She is crooning over it when someone bustles in to say the car is at the door, snatches the jug from the trembling hands, and in a second it lies smashed on the floor. With a cry the old woman rises to her feet, then sinks down in her chair and is still ; she will trouble no one any longer. When the show was over I got a chance to congratulate the woman who had taken the part, and told her how much we had enjoyed her acting.

She shook her head. " Na," she said, " I didna do well. I was feared. They aye tell't me to take two long gentle breaths at the end, but I de'ed ower loud."

In peace-time the Institutes held Sales of Work and Bulb Shows and Rallies, and gave themselves much enjoyment; in time of war they have had an important part to play.

Piles of beautifully knitted articles have been sent to the Army and Navy and Air Force. Parties are made for convalescent men from military hospitals. Much money has been raised for the Red Cross and other good causes. I know of one small Institute that in the last two years has put £1100 into War Savings. A canteen is run by the W.R.I. at Bangour Hospital, a great benefit to friends and relatives of patients who visit frequently that rather inaccessible spot. The Ministry of Information has made it possible for even the most outlying villages to hear speakers from all parts of the globe. A lady from France describes life under German occupation; a laughing, vivacious little Chinese tells of the home she was brought up in, and an Indian in a bright *sari* brings some of the magic of the East into the Institute hall.

In November 1918 came the collapse of Germany, and the Armistice. To many it was a day of hysterical joy and relief, to others it was the saddest of days.

Everyone was unfeignedly thankful that the fighting had ceased—the thought that no more people were being killed seemed to remove a weight that had been lying for years—but it made many of us realise, as we had not done before, how irrevocable was our loss. Other women's men would come home rejoicing, bringing their sheaves with them—but not ours. The Bible words were true, the sound of the weeping drowned the noise of the shouting.

I felt that when I went down to my district to see a

woman who had lost a second son only the week before. She told me, "I was at the back beatin' ma rug when I heard the noise. 'What is't?' I asked. They tell't me, 'It's Peace.' I came in and shut the doors and the windows so that I wouldna hear the bells mocking me."

CHAPTER XII

" I should like to set up my tabernacle here. . . . I am content."
                                                        CHARLES LAMB.

THE brave new world that Peace brought was full of
perplexities and problems that seemed insoluble.
Disabled men were going from door to door begging
householders to buy writing-pads or brushes.   In the cities
men with bars of colours on their shabby coats stood
patiently in the streets, holding trays with matches or small
cheap toys, while others sang and played and went round
with a cap.   The land for heroes to live in that they had
been promised was not in sight, and they must have
thought nostalgically of the trenches—there at least they
had been wanted.

Some of those men may have been lazy and unwilling,
but many of them, eager to work, could find no job, and
were driven to stand on the street by the sight of hungry
children and despairing wives.

Still, we were at peace, families were once more united,
and to many the years between 1918-39 were among the
happiest of their lives.   It was so with J. B.   In 1919 he
sold his house in Portland Place, feeling that it was hardly
fair to bring up in a city children who were such country
lovers.   And as he himself felt an intense craving for a
country life, Susie and he started at once on their quest,
and after looking at all sorts of possible and impossible
houses found one four miles from Oxford, on the hill
above Old Marston, the little manor-house of Elsfield.

From his childhood John had loved a house by the
roadside, and Elsfield seemed just what he wanted.   The
front door opened from the village street on an austere
black and white hall, with a glass door on the left leading

165

to the rose-garden. All the principal rooms looked out on wide lawns sloping down to the water-meadows of the Cherwell, and across some thirty miles of woods and fields to the dim ridges above Stow-in-the-Wold.

Though so near Oxford, Elsfield village remains completely unspoiled. There are no bungalows, a bus once a week or so, the only shop the post-office. All round are lovely villages—Woodeaton, Beckley, Islip.

It was an ideal place, for they were within easy distance of London and yet perfectly secluded.

Much had to be done to the house in the way of bathrooms and running water in the bedrooms, and while the workmen were occupying it the whole family came to Broughton and spent the summer and autumn at Gala Lodge.

Mother, Walter, and I stayed in Mother's old home, Broughton Green, now alas ! sadly changed. Certainly it had needed new plumbing, but what possessed us to let an architect work his wicked will on it I cannot imagine. All the things that gave the house character had been removed. The high steep roof was gone ; the garrets (Frizzel's End, beloved of our childhood) ; the stair with its shallow steps and graceful banister had been replaced by a thing of pitch pine. The small greenish glass panes in the window, that made everything outside look unreal, had been taken out for a stained-glass monstrosity.

Instead of a nest of little rooms there were now a few good-sized ones. True, the upstairs sitting-room with its three windows was a singularly pleasant place. In this room I spent my mornings writing, companioned by J. B. (when he had not to be in Edinburgh at Nelson's), who had no peaceful place to write in Gala Lodge.

He was writing the history of the South African Forces in the war. I was writing *Penny Plain*.

We each chose our own window. John said he wanted to look out at the Catscleugh, I preferred the Drummelzier hills.

It was a wonderful help to have a companion who could tell me how to spell, and could always give me the right words of a quotation. To J. B., who never put pen to paper till he saw a whole book in his mind, it was a continual amusement to see me sitting down before a pile of paper without an idea what I meant to write about. Somehow ideas came, but inspiration never visited me. I simply wrote doggedly so many words a day, counting them every little while to see if I had got the necessary number.

Sometimes I would giggle to myself as I wrote, and John would come and look over my shoulder, saying :

" Making a joke, Nan-pudge ? Let me see."

Every hour or so he would rise and light his pipe, remarking that he didn't know how anyone could write without such an aid to thought, and I was only too glad to stop work too, and have a talk.

My love of quotations always exasperated him. It was largely laziness on my part. When writing *The Proper Place* I found a most apposite passage in " Q " about Elizabeth of Bohemia, the Queen of Hearts, which I simply lifted in bodily.

When I sent the finished MSS. to John he was furious.

" This," he wrote, " is sheer superfluity of naughtiness. *Take out* that chunk of ' Q,' and write the scene in your own words."

Descriptions are always a worry to me, and in *The Proper Place* I felt that to describe the drawing-room in the old house of Rutherford, with the picture framed in the panelling above the fireplace, was quite beyond my powers, so I told John what I wanted to convey and he put it into words for me. I did not feel it was cheating, because I was certain no one could mistake his writing for my wood-notes wild. I knew it was like a patch of brocade on a stuff garment, but that there was such a patch gave me great pride and satisfaction.

There must have been, I daresay, some rather strained times that summer, for Gala Lodge was too small to house comfortably a family of six, and servants, especially as the children seized the opportunity to indulge in whooping-cough. John also developed a sort of sympathetic whoop, and the limit was felt to have been reached one night when a cow in a field near the house laid its head on the fence and joined in the chorus.

It happened to be a marvellous summer, day after day of sunshine, which we often spent picnicking in some green glen. Almost every afternoon the whole family came to tea with us at Broughton Green. The housekeeper there was a famous baker and grudged no trouble, and very often friends from a distance walked over or bicycled—petrol was scarce then as now—so our parties were apt to be large. John and Susie would arrive with the two older children, and later Nanny with the two little ones. One of the children had a passion for giving presents; he brought every day some small offering for 'Gran.' One afternoon Nanny had nothing to give him, and there was a scene of rage and despair. It was with difficulty that he was persuaded to accompany the party, and everyone wondered how he would comport himself. We need not have feared. He walked straight up to my mother, and said in a kindly, patronising voice, "Well, Gran, did you like the jam-cake I brought you yesterday?"

(I have so often wanted to remind people of my former generosity when in temporary embarrassment.)

The children's days were full of 'ploys.' The animals were an endless interest, puppies, kittens, calves, and pet lambs. They invited people to come and see the 'wee calfie,' in broad Border Scots. Some kind friends lent them a little cart, with a donkey called 'Mrs. Kruger' to draw it, which gave them immense pleasure. 'Mrs. Kruger' was a lovable but slightly malicious animal. If the children annoyed her she deliberately tramped on their bare sandalled feet with her little sharp hoofs, and she was not above biting them when they fed her with her favourite caramels. But they loved her devotedly, and the morning she went back to her home at Dawyck, because the children were returning to England, her shaggy coat was wet with the tears shed over her.

The children had a passion for trains, and got a splendid view of our little branch line from Gala Lodge. Their favourite was the afternoon train. As one of them told me, "That little train's the hero of the day, he doesn't mind how many trucks he has to pull." The great excitement was to wait at the level-crossing when I was returning from a day in Peebles by 'the hero of the day,' and search in the grass for small prize-packets which I threw out to them from the carriage window.

A railway strike occurred that September, and one of the boys had the delirious excitement of riding to Peebles with his father in an engine, and being permitted to make it whistle. He accosted everyone he met with ,"D-did you hear the engine whistle? It was me that did it," and in the exuberance of his gratitude he kissed the grimy hand of the engine-driver.

It was a pleasure for John that summer to see something of his relatives at Broughton, Mother's sister and brothers.

'Antaggie,' having nobly given up her house to John and his family, stayed with us at Broughton Green, and kept rather an anxious eye on her property.

Two of our uncles, looked after by an old housekeeper,

led a peaceful existence on their moorland farm. Uncle Jim, the younger of the two, was a great favourite with us. He had a witty tongue, and was excellent company. Uncle John was a sort of saint, a good sort of saint. He was a pillar of the church at Broughton, a Liberal in politics, and a die-hard Tory by nature. Every Sunday, no matter what the weather was, the couple came down in their dog-cart to church. (Nothing would have induced them to buy a car, they held that everything had gone wrong since the internal combustion engine had been invented.) As punctual as Big Ben came the clip-clop of their horse's feet just as the church-bell began to ring.

The youngest brother, the only one who married, marched much more with the times, took his part in public life, and was widely known and popular. No one could sing a Scots song better than he could.

J. B. greatly enjoyed a talk with the three brothers, and was indebted to them for many a good story and expressive Scots idiom.

There was no gas at Broughton, nor (unless you made it yourself) electricity, so we had to depend on paraffin lamps.

It is Charles Lamb, I think, who says that the best books need lamp-light for their complete enjoyment, and there is something in the warm mellow light of a lamp that electricity cannot give.

" I am not much of a friend," he goes on to say, " to open-air reading," and one could not enjoy such a gentle writer, say, on the moors, though I like to read R. L. S. to the accompaniment of a burn and the cry of a whaup and a ' great rooty sweetness of bogs.' But he himself has a delightful description of lamp-light reading. In *Memories and Portraits* he describes coming in from a patrol on the hills with the shepherd, and sitting down to a long lamp-lit evening by the fire with the *Vicomte*, and every now and again he would rise and pull aside the blind and see the snow and the glittering hollies in the garden, and the moonlight on the white hills, then he would turn back to the crowded field of life on the page of his book.

The evenings were our peaceful time that autumn. When the children were asleep in bed, and John and Susie had eaten their dinner quietly by themselves, they nearly always walked over to drink coffee and spend the rest of the evening with us. The lamps lit, the curtains undrawn that we might see the great yellow moon come up over Ratchill, we sat and talked, or John read aloud. Very often Walter managed to come up from Peebles for the night, and that made it perfect.

It has always been a grief to me that so much of what we read and enjoy we forget, and that lamp-lit autumn seemed the time to go back to old friends.

My choice was Neil Munro. When I read his book *The Lost Pibroch* as a young girl, it enchanted me, and each new book of his that came out I read, and meant to read again and again. There they were, safely behind glass doors in the old book-case by the fire, and when I dusted them—always my job at spring-cleaning time—I promised myself that before another spring I would re-read them all. So I brought from Peebles my two favourites, *The New Road* and *John Splendid*. The former is perhaps the best book Neil Munro wrote. John held that it would live as one of the greatest of Scots novels, but *John Splendid* has a haunting charm, and we found it was a perfect book to read aloud. From the beginning when the writer comes back to Inneraora (Inveraray) from the German wars and recalls how he had asked his friend Gavin how he would like best to go into Inneraora when his time came (" Poor

Gavin, good Gavin, he came home no way at all to his mother and his mountains—"), the book is steeped in poetry.

There are passages, like the one beginning "I know corries in Argyll that whisper silken to the winds . . .," of breath-taking beauty, and John Splendid himself ('a kind of a Campbell'), who never spoke the bare truth except to an enemy, whose voice had a note of fondling in it that was like a salve for distress, who was so gallant, and yet had moments of meanness and cowardice!

Who having read could forget his farewell to the blind widow in Glencoe who sheltered him and his friend for a night when they were fleeing on the mountains? They heard as they were leaving that the woman's husband had died a day or two before of the plague. It was more than John Splendid, with his horror of infection, could stand up to.

The blind woman was holding out her hand, and, murmuring that his thong was loose, he bent down to his shoe, but Master Gordon, the narrow and harsh minister, stepped forward and without a word took the woman's hand in his, wrung it with great warmth, then lifting the fingers to his lips softly kissed them and turned away.

"'Oh,' said the woman, with tears welling to her poor eyes, 'oh, Clan Campbell, I'll never call ye down. Ye may have the guile men claim for you, but ye have the way with a widow's heart.'

"John Splendid said never a word."

Neil Munro was only one of the many writers with whom we renewed acquaintance in those peaceful evenings. We were all sorry when an end came to our time together at Broughton. John and his family went south in the end of October, while Mother and Walter and I returned to Peebles.

CHAPTER XIII

EVERY April, after 1919, we took Mother to France to visit Alastair's grave in Duisans Cemetery. We always had, also, directions how to find the graves of other Peeblesshire men whose relations were not able to visit France, and who longed, naturally, for particulars and perhaps a photograph of the place, so in time we saw practically the whole battle area.

When we saw Ypres for the first time it was literally levelled to the ground. The Cloth Hall was a mere ghostly shadow. As we looked at it in that snowy twilight, with a wind moaning among the ruins, it seemed the last word in desolation.

We stayed the night in a hotel with a resounding name, claiming to have a hall of baths. As a matter of fact it was a frail shanty, with slips of bedrooms divided by thin boards through which every whisper was heard. (Mine had for decoration a General's brass hat!) As for baths, the only water anywhere near appeared to be in the moat.

[About ten years later we were again in Ypres. We stayed in a most comfortable hotel run by an Englishman. The town, including the Cloth Hall, had been entirely rebuilt, and we found that the inhabitants considered it a great improvement on the old one, which our young chambermaid dismissed as ' Very ancient.']

We left the next morning and motored to Arras across the Vimy Ridge. Everything seemed to be just as it had been left when the Armistice was declared: a churned-up sea of mud, with trenches littered with tin hats and gum-boots, and miles of rusty barbed wire. It lay like that for years. I remember once on the road from Albert to Arras our chauffeur stopped at a hillock on the roadside. This, he told us, was the famous Butte de Warlencourt, which men had died by thousands to take and hold. On the summit were three tall crosses—like Calvary. Two men were also standing looking at it. Evidently they knew it well, and one turning to the other said, "D'you see? There are cowslips growing in the shell-holes."

Arras, when we reached it, seemed a town of ghosts. Walter and I walked at nightfall through a street of ruined houses. People seemed to be living in the cellars, for we heard the cry of a tiny baby. The town cemetery was an eerie sight, for the graves had been blown open by shell-fire, the bell-tower was lying in ruins and the bell, balanced on a piece of fallen masonry, was reverberating faintly in the wind.

The hotel we stayed in was ghostly too. A shell had come through Walter's ceiling, which was only partially mended, and he could look up to the sky. Mother and I shared a room hung with tapestry, behind which rats squeaked and scraped. But there was no ghostliness, when we drove out the next morning to the little village of Duisans and the cemetery there. It was a peaceful, upland place, with larks singing high overhead, and daffodils blowing in the grass.

It was bare at first, but as the years passed the wooden crosses were replaced by stones, green turf carpeted the place, and flowers grew everywhere. Alastair was one of the first to be laid there, but when we knew it there were thousands of graves.

We always took out special flowers to plant on Alastair's grave, and Gervase Maude's. Alastair and he had probably never seen each other in life, but the fact that they had died together made a link between us and Gervase's parents.

Gervase was their only, adored child, and his loss was too much for his mother. War has many casualties that are not listed.

The years from 1920-37 were good years for us, filled with a multitude of events that make a bright-coloured tapestry of memories. There were, of course, alarms and excursions, sudden illnesses and accidents among the children, which no family is safe from, but on the whole they were placid years, full of content. Always the children came to us for the summer. When the faithful Nanny who had brought them all up had to leave for health reasons the two little boys had Elsie to look after them, a young but most dependable girl, the daughter of Mrs. Charlett at Elsfield. She and her charges stayed at Broughton Green with Maggie, the housekeeper, and spent their days with us and the two older children at Gala Lodge.

By this time gentle 'Antaggie' had gone (her husband had died some years before), leaving the world poorer for many. We missed her badly at Gala Lodge. She had such a delightfully soothing way of saying when we were worried about anything, " Try not to think about it, dear." That was her attitude to life.

One summer the youngest boy became suddenly ill with some sort of blood-poisoning and we had to rush him in to Edinburgh to a specialist. It was a nightmare excursion because Mother and Elsie and I were rent with anxiety. The second boy described it in a postcard to his mother :

" We went for a dreive yesterday. I was sik over O Dougal's skirt."

One year, when their parents had gone on a trip to the States and Canada, the two younger boys were with us in Peebles, and made their first acquaintance with school. They were very polite children, and when one of them was asked by the teacher to tell her what something was, he said pleasantly, " I would tell you in a minute if I knew."

The years for me were punctuated by the books I wrote —one about every two years. Writing, I think, must be rather like drug-taking, once you begin you've got to go on. It was a great effort to me to write, and I don't quite know why I went on doing it. Certainly the money was very useful, and, as giving is a form of self-indulgence with me, I can do with a lot, but it was not entirely the money. Perhaps it was because so many people seemed to get pleasure from one's books one felt one must not fail them —like the loathly Imogen in *Valerie Upton*, who said, " They *need* my letters " !

Had I been writing to earn my bread it is probable that I would have worked better. It was interesting to read in Sir Walter Scott's *Diary* that he never worked well at a serial if he were too far ahead of the printers. He said he was like an old horse that needed the *dunt* of the cart behind him to keep him going.

It was always a great relief to get a book finished and sent off to J. B. to be 'vetted,' and he never failed in encouraging me. Sir Ernest Hodder-Williams had the typescript of *Penny Plain* bound and sent to Mother. It is amusing to see how John blue-pencilled the passages that were too 'incorrigibly noble,' and dealt relentlessly with the 'quotes.' Mother was inclined to be indignant and wondered how he could possibly have disapproved of such highly moral utterances.

At home I was never encouraged to take myself or my writing seriously. Nobody minded interrupting me. I had not even a room of my own. When strangers came and asked in hushed tones, " *May* we see where you write your books ? " I could only reply, " Oh—just all about." A small table beside the fire in the family living-room was my favourite place in winter, and general conversation was no bar to my literary efforts. I joined in and wrote at the same time, which perhaps accounts for the sort of work I produced.

In the end it was Susie who insisted I must have a place where I would be free of interruption, and Walter gave me a room in a house opposite our own, which he had taken for extra office-space.

It was, I found, a great relief to be free of people, and be able to look forward to some hours of peace, but, it is to be confessed, no one noticed any improvement in the quality of my work.

Some of my books I almost enjoyed writing—*Pink Sugar*, which was all about Broughton and the children. In *The Proper Place* I became so much attached to my characters that I wrote a second book about them—*The Day of Small Things*, and it was like getting home to find myself in the Harbour House again with Lady Jane and Nicole.

In *Ann and Her Mother* I wrote my mother's Life. (She had already written it herself, in pencil, in a tuppeny notebook, but that didn't count.)

It was not to be expected that it could be as popular as a story—a simple record of small happenings. In Oliver Goldsmith I found a good foreword for it: "In this age of opulence and refinement whom can such a character please? Such as are fond of high life will turn in disdain from the simplicity of a country fireside. Such as mistake ribaldry for humour will find no wit in this harmless conversation: such as have been taught to deride religion will laugh at one whose chief stores of comfort are drawn from futurity."

Naturally Mother took a great interest in how her 'Life' was received. In this world there must be quite a lot of people who like simple goodness, for the book has con-

tinued to sell in various editions up to the present day—
a matter of two-and-twenty years.

A soldier's wife (unknown to me) wrote from India
lately and told me that when she was going into hospital
to have her first baby, feeling lonely and far from home, she
took with her for comfort *Ann and Her Mother*.

One result of my writing was that I was continually
being asked to open Bazaars and Sales of Work, and speak
at luncheons and public dinners. Wherever I went Mother
accompanied me, going long train journeys, motoring
many miles, and without her it would have been a dreary
business, for she was ready to enjoy everything.

The church had always been her chief interest, and
going to sales and other functions, meeting people with
whom she had much in common, and feeling that we were
helping good causes a little, pleased her mightily.

Now and again she was rather trying, remarking as we
set off on some trek, " I do hope you have something fresh
today," to which I coldly replied that I was not a fish-
monger.

Sometimes she was pleased with my efforts, sometimes
not. One chairman, introducing me, said he was sure
that whatever I spoke about I would make it amusing,
which had the effect of reducing me to a depth of dullness
hitherto unplumbed.

Mother laughed as we drove away, saying " That poor
man will be sorry he mentioned humour. What a drab
speech ! "

Sometimes I opened three different things in a day, and
it became quite expensive, as one had either to give a
donation or buy largely. I was the one who spoke, but
the audience, I am sure, thought as much of Mother's presence as mine. We preferred to go to struggling concerns,
the wealthy ones were so complacent, so well pleased with

themselves and their efforts. In many cases we found that the poorer the people, the greater the enthusiasm.

One December afternoon I specially remember. The church we were going to was down near the Clyde in Glasgow; the rain was pouring steadily on the crowds of shabby people doing their Saturday shopping, and what little light there was was quickly going. We felt we were in for a grim afternoon, but when we reached the hall we knew at once that all was well. The place was gay with colour, and every face beamed with pride at the way they had managed to stock their stalls. The object of the sale was a new boiler for the heating apparatus, and the chairman in his speech recalled that at one time the church had had no heating, and when a meeting was called to discuss it an old elder rose and said, " If the minister preaches as he ought, no further heating is required ! "

" It's like Knox's," Mother said, and she could give no greater praise.

Country places we found rather more stolid and difficult to rouse, but in one place the ice was broken for us by a turkey-cock. A farmer had sent it, and it was tethered just in front of the platform. Every time I paused in my speech, it gobbled, and every time it gobbled the people yelled with laughter. After that, when we went to a country sale, I looked hopefully for a turkey-cock, but never again, alas !

Lecturing was another job I had to undertake. A ten-minutes' speech to people standing treading on each other at a crowded sale is never an easy thing to do well, but lecturing is a different matter. Then the audience is comfortably seated, and you have them at your mercy for at least an hour.

Sir Walter Raleigh seems to have had bad luck in audiences : " I never had such a job—a sea of wooden faces, not a smile in them. I glared wildly among them, and caught what I thought was a sympathetic expression on a woman's face, but just then she yawned. Then I fixed upon a man and he got up and went out. It was awful!"

I, too, have found myself searching for a responsive face to speak to. If only an audience realised what it means to a speaker, if they look a little pleased to be there—not merely patient and enduring!

Once, at an afternoon drawing-room meeting, I glanced round and was disgusted at the rows of apathetic faces turned to a most accomplished woman speaker. Suddenly in a mirror I got a glimpse of my own face—long, dull, with lack-lustre eyes. Since then I have always tried at a meeting to sit with a bright, interested, if slightly galvanised expression, in case of discouraging any speaker who might glance my way. But given the sort of audience that holds you up and make you feel you are swimming freely in a wide salt sea and not struggling in a muddy pond, lecturing can be great fun.

On one occasion when I wanted to raise some money for a local effort I lectured for a fee—in Chester and Blackpool and Liverpool. English audiences I found delightfully easy to talk to, but the thought of the fee made me self-conscious and I kept wondering if I were worth it.

Through those years John was working hard and happily. His health, except at intervals, was never very good, but he refused to let it master him, and somehow managed to keep on top of his condition. "A light affliction," he would say when he was sympathised with. Now and again he was forced to take a rest. He was much better after some weeks in the Black Forest under a German doctor. A new treatment always helped him for a little, and he never allowed himself to expect more. When one thinks that his inside was rarely quite comfortable, it is surprising how little irritable he was, and work and the society of his friends often made him forget it entirely for the time being.

Five days a week he went to London. He had to leave by the early morning train, but he always had time to run up to the nursery—which was on a level with the swaying tops of the elm trees, so that one could almost look into the rooks' nests—and pat the gilt heads of his two younger sons as they sat urbanely eating porridge. He much preferred travelling third-class, because of the company, and always had tales to tell us of the interesting people he met— ' the Noblest Man in the Pig Trade ' and many others. At last Susie compelled him to travel first, that he might have more room and a more restful journey, but he often regretted his former friends.

The days in London were very full, and at home he was writing continuously. The extraordinary thing was he never seemed in the very least oppressed with work, nor even very busy. He sat at his side of the big writing-table in the library—Susie had the other side—and wrote without appearing to be disturbed by the clamour of laughter and talk that went on around him. He never worked after dinner, but talked or read aloud, and went off early to bed. He was an excellent sleeper.

The secret was that he was exact about everything and never wasted a minute. When he was writing Lord Minto's Life he said to us one evening, " I'll finish Minto tomorrow at eleven o'clock." As the clock struck eleven the next morning he laid down his pen—and at eleven-fifteen he had begun another book !

Susie and I looked at him with some distaste. To us, to whom writing was such a labour, the ease with which he wrote seemed hardly human, and almost insulting.

He had learned to love the countryside round Oxford when at Brasenose, and now that it was his home it meant much to him. Minster Lovell gave him the idea for *The Blanket of the Dark*. a legend about Dr. Johnson and the Jacobites made him write *Midwinter*, and all the time he was writing the Hannay books. Sometimes he cut himself shaving through chuckling at some cantrip of the Gorbals Die-Hards and Dickson McCunn that had come into his head.

J. B. always felt that they had done a wise thing in deciding to be country dwellers. Elsfield was a delight to them all. He and Susie spent strenuous hours working in the garden. There was a pond, and beneath it a little glade with a burn running through it, and they determined to make this a sort of water-garden. The children had any amount of space, and a wealth of outhouses to play in, not to speak of a twelfth-century barn which, when they grew older, John fitted up as a small hall, with a stage and everything complete.

In one of the outhouses the three boys started a bank. Painted on the door was the legend ' Buchan Bros.' We were all asked to put some money into it—half a crown was, I think, the sum suggested—and we received in return a neat little cheque-book. But it was not a dependable bank : we never saw our half-crowns again.

Elsfield always seemed to me a singularly happy home, and it helped to make a happy village.

Mrs. Charlett, the cook, instead of being a firebrand as so many good cooks are, was a sort of benediction in the place. She was a widow, and at one time had three of her family working with her at Elsfield. John, coming in from a tramp on a wet day, liked to go round by the basement with his wet coat, and find Mrs. Charlett, with her benign face and comfortable presence, presiding over a tea-party which included the postman and the carrier. That, he said, was the nice thing about having a house by the side of the road ; people could be cheered on their way.

John cheered many people on their way, giving not only money but, what meant much more to him, time. He never grudged writing letters and interviewing people about jobs during the difficult years that lay between the Wars, when so many young men were compelled to be idle. When misfortune overtook a friend he was there, and willing to help to his uttermost. After he had gone, we were unhappily conscious that many of whom we knew nothing must be missing bitterly his help and encouragement.

The Manor was the place the villagers went to for advice or help in a difficulty. The men working on the place were all friends of the boys, and to this day their letters home always contain affectionate messages of remembrance to them. Amos Webb, the chauffeur, was part of the Elsfield background. His smiling face at the station when we arrived on a visit was the first of our welcome. It was delightful to see the same smile in Canada. He went out with John and was with him all the time, dying a few months after his master.

Many people thought it strange that J. B. had wanted to be buried in Elsfield, and not in his own Tweeddale, but it was very natural. The happiest years of his life had been spent there, there he had seen his children grow up ; everyone in the place was his friend, and it is very fitting that close beside him lies Amos Webb—'that good man of such dear memory.'

CHAPTER XIV

" Alas ! Poor Queen.
Consider the way she had to go,
Think of the hungry snare,
The net she herself had woven,
Aware or unaware,
Of the dancing feet grown still,
The blinded eyes.—
Queens should be cold and wise,
And she loved little things,
    Parrots
And red-legged partridges
And the golden fishes of the Duc de Guise
And the pigeon with the blue ruff
She had from Monsieur d'Elbœuf."

MARION ANGUS.

IN 1927 J. B. was invited to stand as Unionist candidate
for the Scottish Universities. It was an ideal constituency for him to represent, needing no travelling about
nor talking, no fishing for votes, and he frankly enjoyed
his time at Westminster. Having many friends in all
parties he was at home from the first. His maiden-speech
(I did not hear it) was considered a great success, though
some complained that he spoke in ' a wailing pulpit mono-
tone.' It is true that if he started off on a wrong note he
did wail, but when he was completely at ease with his
subject and his audience he could speak delightfully.

At the time of the Scott Centenary celebrations, after
receiving, along with others, the Freedom of Selkirk, he
spoke to a large gathering on Sir Walter. Nothing could
have been better : it was a man talking to his friends about
a mutual friend greatly beloved. Hugh Walpole said of
his *Life of Scott* that it seemed to be written with the hand
of Scott resting on the writer's shoulder, and there was the
same feeling of intimacy about the speech.

In Scotland that summer there were all manner of Scott celebrations, and Peebles had quite a good one. Dr. Clement Gunn (father of Winifred Gunn who wrote the play, *Scott of Abbotsford*) gave the oration, and then the curtain went up on what looked like a gigantic open book, and from the pages of this book, one by one, characters from Scott's novels emerged and said their say : Meg Merrilies, Diana Vernon, Jeanie Deans, Meg Dods, Graham of Claverhouse, Cuddie Headrigg, and others.

J. B. wrote a short sketch for the occasion. Scott (played by John) was sitting busily writing when his henchman, Tom Purdie, came in to say that a hoodie-crow had built its nest in one of the oak-trees planted by Scott. This event delights the Laird of Abbotsford, and he forgets the weary task before him as he and his man discuss it at length. Tom Purdie goes out, and presently the tired man at his desk drops asleep, his pen falling from his hand ; and as he sleeps his characters steal in and stand round their creator. It was very effectively produced by William Crichton, the Scottish actor and broadcaster.

Being in Parliament naturally meant a great deal of extra work for John. In the election of 1932, after he had made a lot of speeches up and down the country (not to speak of fishing in Highland rivers) he had a bad bout of his duodenal trouble and was in bed for several weeks, but no sooner was he allowed up than he began again to work with energy unabated.

In the beginning of April 1933, Susie and I were in London for a few days with the children. Alice was studying at the R.A.D.A., Johnny was at Brasenose (following his father and his uncle), the two younger boys were at Eton. One evening we had all been to *Richard of Bordeaux* and were eagerly discussing it, when a note came in from John to Susie which she glanced at and put in her bag. Later she told me that John had been asked to go as Lord High Commissioner to the General Assembly of the Church of Scotland, but that nothing was to be said about it till a certain date. The papers, however, got it before that date, and several of them rang up my mother at Peebles to know what she thought of it.

As it happened Mother was alone that evening, sitting in Walter's study where the telephone was, and got the whole brunt of the attack. Having heard nothing about it from John she naturally assumed that it was a mistake, and said so, but when the fourth paper rang up she began to get annoyed. " Please don't say that again," she said firmly, " it isn't true." And went to bed.

The Assembly had always meant much to Mother. When she was lying very ill in London Sir Almroth Wright said to John, " She is very anxious to be present at some assembly in May, but she isn't fit to go to a dance ! " It was the greatest dissipation of her life to stay in a Princes Street Hotel, to attend Missionary Breakfasts, sit for long hours in the Moderator's Gallery listening to debates, rush out for hurried luncheons and back again. In the evenings there were numerous meetings, varied by the Moderator's Reception, and a Reception at Holyrood.

Her happiest assemblies were of course in Father's life-time, but she put up with me as a companion for many years, and in time I enjoyed it almost as much as she did, I suppose because her pleasure was infectious. That her son should represent the King at her beloved Assembly seemed to her at first almost too dizzy an honour, but John made her feel that he needed her, and that she had a part in it. He consulted her about his speech at the opening, and her face was a study as she listened to him telling of the four men who had most influenced his youth, William Welsh, the Free Church minister of Broughton ; Norman

Walker of the old Fife days ; Ralph Smith of John Knox's, Glasgow ; and his own father.

To me the wonder of the thing was to live in Holyrood-house. Most of us have been sightseers in our time in that ancient palace, going round, meek and footsore after a guide, kept in our place by plush ropes and warnings not to touch, but to see behind the scenes, guides and the public shut out ; to have one's abode there, to be able to go up the twisting staircase and stand alone in Queen Mary's room—the Queen who loved little things—for eleven days to live in history, it was as if one had been offered a lease of Fairyland.

The only thing that troubled me was the thought of the nights. Someone wrote in the *Glasgow Herald* of " Haunted Nights in Holyrood," and asked :

" Ladies-in-waiting, when you lie awake o' nights upon whom do your thoughts most dwell ? Upon fair Margaret of England shivering in draughts of a strange country and hearkening fearfully to a gale blowing up from the Forth, or upon the four Marys bending over their embroidery the while Rizzio makes in their ears sweet music ?

" Is it the Queen in the pride of her youth and beauty, you see gliding along the twisting corridors, or is it the woman whom love betrayed you see stealing fearfully down the palace steps, and looking her last upon the cold grey walls ? . . . But perhaps the ladies-in-waiting upon the wife of the Lord High Commissioner do not lie awake at night. Perhaps they sleep soundly within the old historic walls. Only at times strange dreams must visit them, dreams that they can no more recall at waking than you can recall the refrain of a forgotten song. But part of the sheen of those dreams remains to haunt them, a sheen composed of scarlet and purple, of love and the flash of a broadsword."

Most assuredly strange dreams would have visited me, had I had to sleep alone far from human aid, but owing to Susie's thoughtfulness I cosily shared my mother's room, which was next that of ' Their Graces.'

J. B. had chosen for his chaplain his old friend Charles Dick, author of that delightful book *Highways and Byways of Galloway*, and now a minister in Shetland. They had been at school and college together and Charles had often spent his holidays with us, when we all scoured the hills together. On one occasion he and John bicycled to Penicuik to call on S. R. Crockett, the novelist. The letter of introduction (which they had got from an old minister in the vicinity) explained their intrusion by the remark—" These young men are addicted to literature." It sounded so much worse than drink !

It is the custom for the Lord High Commissioner and his guests to gather for prayers at nine o'clock every morning in the drawing-room opening from the Throne-room. I knew Mother was looking forward to this, and I said to Charles (rather smugly), that though all the guests might not avail themselves of the privilege, he might be quite sure that Mother and I would be there.

There was a large dinner-party after the ceremony of Presenting the Keys of the City, and we went to bed that first night rather weary. Everything in our room had been beautifully tidied away, and we wondered if we ought to look for what we meant to put on in the morning, but I said that Amy (Susie's maid), who was to look after us, would know just where they were and we had better leave it to her.

I had brought *The Queen's Qhair* with me to re-read in Mary's own palace, and, waking early, I lay in great content. Mother, busy with her devotional books (she carried about a dozen wherever she went), remarked at intervals that she thought we ought to get up, but I, deep in my book, murmured that we couldn't get up till we were called. I was relying on Amy, but, had I known it, Amy had been reft away to another floor to look after a guest in difficulties, so we never were called.

John looked in on his way back from his bath, and had I not been utterly bemused I would have realised that if he were up we should be up too.

Then Alice dashed in, morning-bright, shouting, " Are you ready for prayers ? "

Mother gave a wail of utter anguish. We bounded up, but our garments had been so successfully hidden that we could not find what we wanted, and Mother kept on moaning, " Oh, how *could* you do it ? "

I did feel very bad about it, and when at last, only sketchily washed and partially clothed, we reached the door of the Throne-room we met the company filing out to breakfast.

Mother was in no mood for persiflage, and when an Eminent Person suggested archly that a court-martial after breakfast was indicated she looked at him stonily.

But the thrill of driving through Edinburgh with bands playing and horses prancing, and a salute of twenty-one guns booming from the castle, made her forget the day's bad beginning.

It was the first time that a son of the Manse had held office as Lord High Commissioner. As John told the great audience in the Assembly Hall, he was one of themselves : he had in his bones the traditions of Scottish Presbyterianism, and his upbringing had been in the historic Free Church.

We had been brought up to regard 1843 as the year of one of the greatest events in Scotland's history, the year of the Disruption, when 474 ministers of the Church of

Scotland walked out, giving up all they possessed of ecclesiastical endowment, and going literally into the wilderness that they might have liberty to worship as they thought best.

The leaders of this tremendous adventure must have been made of stern stuff. As a child I used to look at their photographs in my mother's album. Dr. Chalmers, Dr. Guthrie, Dr. Begg and others—disinheriting countenances some of them had.

We were often told the story of Dr. Begg's visit to our manse. The parents had to go out, and left their guest reading by the study fire. John had looked in and, seeing him alone, lugged from a low shelf a large volume for his entertainment. Dr. Begg told him not to bring any more, but John persisted with a second and a third. Then Dr. Begg beat him, and when Mother came in announced, " I have had dealings with your son."

My job at Holyroodhouse was to be a sort of understudy to Lady Kinross, who was Lady-in-waiting, and I found it a liberal education to see how beautifully she did it. Gracious and sweet to everyone, she created a delightfully friendly atmosphere which made everything go happily. J. B. himself was always a good mixer and had an eager welcoming way of greeting everyone brought up to him that was very likeable. " Ringed round with a flame of fair faces, and splendid with swords " he remained perfectly natural.

' Her Grace ' was just what I knew she would be, dignified and gentle, with an amused look at the corners of her mouth.

Mother might be described as a link between the Church and the State, interpreting the one to the other. John felt her to be an enormous help, and when it was all over presented her with a bulky volume, sumptuously bound, into which he had pasted with his own hands, pictures, press-cuttings, letters, and sketches about our time in Holyroodhouse, which he inscribed :

" To my dearest Mother

" This record of what was as much her show as mine."

Alice and some of her friends as Maids-of-honour made a pretty group, and worked hard to make the guests enjoy themselves.

The really important person at Holyroodhouse is the Purse-bearer. On him largely depends the smooth running of everything. (The reason of the name Purse-bearer was never quite clear to me, but he did carry a velvet bag from which on the Sunday we were each given half a crown to put in the church plate.) Besides big luncheon and dinner-parties daily, there is always an evening reception and a garden-party. The last-named entertainment depends for success on the weather, and if the day arranged is wet cannot take place.

One summer when King George V and Queen Mary were holding Court at Holyroodhouse, people were invited from all parts of Scotland to a garden-party. It was a perfect day and all was going merrily when, with dramatic suddenness, the sky darkened and a thunder-storm broke. There was no shelter on the wide lawns ; it was a case of crying on the rocks to cover us, and in a few minutes hundreds of lovely frocks and hats were reduced to pulp. So heavy was the rain that in the car park some of the heavier cars sank in the mud and could not be got out for hours. It was a draggled and discomfited company who sought their homes that night.

But we were fortunate both years to get a bright dry day.

Besides entertaining, the Lord High Commissioner and

his Lady visit hospitals and all manner of charitable insti-
tutions, not to speak of such useful things as the Atholl
Crescent School of Cooking. It was a popular place to
visit, not only because of the interesting things we saw,
but because of the beautiful iced cake we carried away
with us.

J. B. had at least forty speeches to make during his term
of office, as well as his big speeches in the Assembly Hall,
and Susie had many things of her own to do, so we were
all pretty weary sometimes when we gathered for tea in
the west drawing-room that looked out on Arthur's Seat.

That lovely room was a sanctuary, used entirely by the
house-party. There is something so restful about the
economy of its decorations, the exquisite soft colouring of
the faded tapestry, the big wood fires. Here, as everywhere, Mary Queen of Scots pervades the place. Above
the hum of the tea-tables, glancing ironically under her
lashes, she looks across to the portrait of her son James
praying for vengeance on the murderer of his father,
Darnley.

The last night came when we stood in the packed
Assembly Hall and sang :

> " Pray that Jerusalem may have
> Peace and felicity,"

and went down the long flight of stone steps to the quad-
rangle, with friendly hands stretched out on all sides to
wish us God-speed. The next morning the bugles sounded
for the last time as we drove away, while, in the ancient
palace, the blinds were drawn down and the plush ropes
replaced.

Two people will never forget that time in Holyroodhouse, Alice, the Maid-of-Honour, and Brian Fairfax-Lucy,
the A.D.C. Meeting there for the first time, they were
married before the summer was out.

CHAPTER XV

WE were all back in Holyroodhouse the next May, and in some ways the second year was even pleasanter than the first.

It was a particularly gay summer with us, that of 1934, with many people coming and much visiting about. In these restricted war years it seems hardly possible that we thought nothing of motoring thirty or forty miles to lunch with people. Perhaps Mother did too much and over-taxed her strength, for she was suddenly seized with acute asthma, that distressing complaint which had so afflicted her father.

We took her up to Broughton for rest and quiet and she gradually improved, but she never quite got rid of it and every winter was liable to attacks.

In the spring of 1935 the appointment of John as Governor-General of Canada was received by her with mixed feelings. That it was a great honour she quite realised, but she had reached an age when honours do not seem very important—and this one meant separation.

The peerage that followed she regarded with little favour. Her young grandson agreed with her, remarking that he did not like new peerages.

"But this one is for merit," he was reminded, to which he replied, "That makes it worse."

But Mother would have been less than human had she not been touched and pleased by the pleasure and pride her many friends showed in this signal honour, and she thoroughly enjoyed being fêted and made much of.

John and his youngest boy (who was going out to

Canada with his parents for the first year, having finished with Eton and being still too young for Oxford) spent a fortnight with us at Broughton in August, and before they sailed in the end of October the three came to Peebles for a farewell visit.

It had been a strenuous summer for J. B., speeches at numberless functions, people to see, arrangements to make, and he was pretty well worn out before he sailed. The voyage to which he had been looking forward for a rest was one of continual storms, and though he was a good sailor his digestion, as usual in times of strain, gave him trouble.

It was a good thing they had the quiet time in the St. Lawrence, for when they reached Quebec, on the evening of November 2nd, they had to proceed at once to the Senate Chamber of Quebec Parliament Buildings for the ' swearing in ' ceremony. They were all new to the job. John had brought with him as secretary, Shuldham Redfern (whose wife and little boy accompanied him). John Boyle was a military A.D.C., Gordon Rivers-Smith, the naval A.D.C. Susie had taken as Lady-in-Waiting, Beatrice Spencer-Smith, who had been all her life a friend of the children, and had for a time shared Alice's governess at Elsfield, and so was a bit of home.

This was, of course, a full-dress occasion. The Senate Chamber was filled with a representative gathering from all parts of the Dominion.

Nearly five years after this ceremony had taken place I read the following account of it, written by Archdeacon Scott of Quebec :

" When Lord Tweedsmuir entered, accompanied by his aides and a military escort, the audience, of course, rose, and after taking their seats they saw, sitting on the throne, a slight and frail man in Court uniform, almost blinded by a fierce light which beat upon him from a searchlight in the gallery at the end of the Chamber. The ' swearing in ' was carried out, as it always is, with its quaint ceremony. Then came addresses of welcome both in English and French.

" At their conclusion the new Governor-General replied briefly in a quiet, modest manner, expressing his pleasure to be in Canada. He followed up his English speech with one in French, and thus struck a note of sympathy and understanding of the dual nature of the Dominion—which was his to the end.

" Out of the accustomed pageantry surrounding the official installation to his office, emerged the man who for nearly five years went up and down the length and breadth of Canada, going into the wilds, following the track of our early discoverers, and making friends of all with whom he came in contact. His absolute sincerity, his freedom from all self-assertion and the power of his intellect, gave him a dignity wherever he went and in whatsoever function he was engaged, which needed no external trappings to mark him out as a prince among men."

J. B. was anxious that Mother should pay him a visit as soon as possible, so she and I arranged to go in the spring of 1936.

Earlier in that year Johnny—who had gone out to Uganda, in the Colonial service, when he left Oxford—was invalided home after repeated attacks of dysentery. It was a very great disappointment to him as he had liked his work and thoroughly enjoyed the life out there, but there was no help for it : he could not have recovered in that climate. For some time he was a patient in the London Hospital for Tropical Diseases, and then was allowed to go to his grandmother's house at Upper Grosvenor Street.

Mrs. Grosvenor kept open house for the whole family, and they would have been rather desolate without that friendly open door when Elsfield was closed to them.

In the end of February Mother and I went to London and brought Johnny home with us. He was still far from well, but it was a great satisfaction to see how Peebles air seemed to revive him. Every day he was able to walk a little farther, and in the end of March he was well enough to leave for Canada. His parents had had a miserably anxious time for about eight months, as he was sent from one little jungly hospital to another, and their relief was great to have him beside them.

We left in the end of April. Mother was then nearly seventy-nine, but she set off without a tremor, and I was not unduly anxious, knowing her capacity for seeing a thing through without being a trouble to anyone.

It was a bright cold April day when we left Greenock. Walter had motored in with us from Peebles, and Brian Fairfax-Lucy, being in Glasgow for the night, had made time, in his kind way, to come and see us off.

We began to see 'ferlies' just at once, for, sailing down the Firth of Clyde, we met the *Queen Mary*, just launched and looking very regal, doing a trial trip.

We had booked a cabin in the *Duchess of Atholl*, and found when we went on board we had been given not one cabin but two, and a sitting-room. The sitting-room was quite full of flowers and fruit and boxes of chocolates, as well as books and magazines sent by kind friends, some quite unknown to us. Such largesse made us feel that we knew in a small way what it must be like to be a film star.

Before leaving Peebles I had been told, rather threateningly, by a member of the Mothers' Union, "Now, see you look after your mother on that ship," and I replied that it was only too probable that my mother would have to look after me.

And so it proved. We sat at the Captain's table on the first night, but until we reached the St. Lawrence that was the only time I sat at it. Almost at once I gave up the unequal contest.

To lie in bed is really much the best way to get through an Atlantic crossing in cold and stormy weather, and I must say I was supremely happy lying there, warm and comfortable, with lots of reading. If I stayed still I was not seasick, and could even enjoy my meals.

My indomitable little mother went down to every meal. She generally lost her way coming back from the dining-room, and was restored to me by different members of the crew. She spent most of her time writing long letters to her countless friends, and found the days all too short.

We were met at Quebec by Colonel Eric Mackenzie, Alastair, and lovely Didy Battye, who was paying a long visit to Government House. The Governor-General's train had been sent to meet us and that in itself was a great thrill. It consisted of a dining-room, a drawing-room, and several bedrooms, all prettily furnished and most comfortable. After luncheon we explored it all, and then Mother sat down to write letters, being quite unable to resist notepaper with the heading, 'Governor-General's Train.' It was quite late when, rather dazed with new impressions, we arrived at Ottawa.

Government House, or Rideau Hall, is more like a large, comfortable country house than an official residence.

When the Duke of Connaught became Governor-General it was given an imposing new front. We thought it all delightful, but what particularly pleased us was the wealth of flowers. The gardeners there must be very good at their job, for the hall and every room were filled with

197

flowering bulbs, masses of azaleas, bowls of violets, tiny little laburnum trees in pots.

The house is surrounded by wide lawns and gardens, and among the tall trees squirrels and chipmunks play.

It was still almost winter when we arrived, but in the beginning of May it got suddenly warm, and everything rushed out. The tulips burst into bloom almost as one watched them, and I never saw lilac of such a rich dark purple.

One ought to see Ottawa when it is deep in snow, but I like to remember it as we saw it, a leafy Ontario town, happy beside its river. It has an almost perfect site, clustering round the noble buildings on Parliament Hill : the glorious Victory Tower ' topping the trees like a mirage.' What walks we had through the Gatineau Woods, learning the names of the flowers from an ardent botanist—pipsissewa, trailing arbutas, Dutchman's breeches : the thrill of dashing up the Ottawa in a launch, dodging the logs that floated down, and the picnic teas enjoyed when we reached a specially attractive place on its banks !

We were much impressed by the beauty of the outskirts of Ottawa. When we saw houses standing among green laws and fine trees with never a wall or a fence or a hedge between them, we thought discontentedly of the way our own suburbs are all parcelled out, every house hemmed in. The fact that an Englishman's house is his castle does not make for beauty, and one of the few good things the war has done for us is to rid us of a lot of ugly railings.

We had always breakfast alone as a family at Government House, which made a pleasant beginning to the day. Luncheon and dinner were more or less formal meals, guests being practically always present. We had all to gather shortly before a meal in the drawing-room, and when an A.D.C. announced ' Their Excellencies ' the men present bowed and the women curtseyed. It reminded me of the advice of the Duchess to Alice, " Curtsey when you're thinking what to say." The legs of people in Court circles must, one supposes, attain to a great degree of pliability, but mine never seemed to be in the right position at the right moment, and I was always rather surprised to find that I had not disgraced myself by toppling over. As for my mother, she said firmly that hers were not the kind of legs to curtsey, and anyway she was too old to begin, so she only gave ' Their Excellencies ' a kind nod.

As there were often long waits in the drawing-room while dinner-parties were assembling she thought it would be a good place to occupy the time by knitting. On one occasion Colonel Arthur Murray and his clever, charming wife (Faith Celli) came to stay. They had been visiting the Roosevelts and meeting many people, and, tired by their journey, were a little dismayed to arrive to a large dinner-party. When they entered the drawing-room the first thing they noticed was my mother, a tiny figure in grey lace, sitting knitting placidly in the corner of a large sofa, and the sight of her made everything seem so home-like that fatigue was forgotten and they were soon eagerly talking to her about mutual friends on Tweedside.

(Colonel Arthur Murray's ancestor was the Colonel Murray who fought with Wolfe, the first Governor-General of Canada. Murray Bay and the Murray River are called after him.)

One hears much of the kindness and hospitality of the Canadian people, and I can testify to the fact that such reports are not exaggerated, indeed one could say with the Queen of Sheba that the half had not been told.

We arrived knowing no one, and were surprised and delighted to be greeted with gifts of beautiful flowers, welcoming letters, and invitations to stay with people in all parts of the Dominion.

We had only been in Ottawa a week when I was sent off, accompanied by Mother, to speak to the Women's Canadian Club in Toronto. We were to stay with the Lieutenant-Governor and his wife, Dr. and Mrs. Bruce. It was rather an ordeal to go to stay with complete strangers, and speak to an audience whose taste in speeches one had no means of knowing.

The fact that by travelling all night we were arriving before breakfast did not make us feel any happier, and altogether, we felt that this was one of the times that we had to brace ourselves up to live through.

We had no thought of seeing our hostess at such an early hour, but Mrs. Bruce was waiting on the doorstep to greet us. She welcomed us with warmth, gave us breakfast, and piloted us to our rooms up marble staircases on which fell a purple light from stained glass somewhere in the roof. The house was the official residence of the Lieutenant-Governor of Ontario and so grand that we literally slept in marble halls.

His Honour the Lieutenant-Governor was a brilliant surgeon, and the author of several books. His wife was English—they had met in France in the last war—and they had a tall schoolboy son.

It takes more than mere cleverness to make an official residence into a home, and to make ' official ' guests feel like the flowers in May, but Mrs. Bruce did it with ease, and those three days with them in Toronto are a gay and happy memory.

We were shown the sights of that wonderful city, and its beautiful surroundings. Especially were we interested to see the Bruces' real home, a lovely country place where their son could indulge his love for farming.

JOHN AND HIS MOTHER

Taken at Ottawa by Karsh.

We met in the flesh some book-friends, and lunched and talked Peebles with a friend of many years' standing now living in Toronto, and through Mrs. Bruce's kindness had the opportunity of meeting quite a lot of the residents of that conspicuous city.

A Toronto audience I found a particularly easy one to speak to. From the start one felt one was speaking to friends, and their cordiality was most heartening. Perhaps it was because Toronto has a strong Scottish flavour. After I had spoken, many women came to shake hands, saying as they did so, " I'm a Macdonald," or as the case might be, a MacKinnon, a Mackenzie, a MacDougal—till one almost felt one had strayed from Toronto into the Oban Gathering.

Back in Ottawa the time passed all too quickly. Once or twice we went on tour with ' Their Excellencies ' in the Governor-General's train. A particularly interesting trip was to the Niagara district. We saw it with the blossom out, miles and miles of it ; a sight to dream of.

It is a lovely countryside round Niagara, low hills, fat farm-lands dotted with villages and friendly spires. In order that we (Mother and I) should see as much as possible, some kind people brought their car and drove us round for a whole day, while ' Their Excellencies ' did official things in the towns. (We were much intrigued to find that we were followed all the way by a car containing two ' Mounties.')

We were interested to see the oldest house in Ontario, a lonely farm-house which had been there when Laura Secord, driving her cow to graze past the unsuspecting American sentries, warned the British of the attack on Beaver Dam. We saw the monument to that great Canadian soldier, General Brock. And we saw the Niagara Falls.

That world's wonder quite came up to one's expectations. Indeed, there was a width and grandeur about the Falls that surpassed any idea one had formed, but it was rather startling to come upon the Falls almost in the midst of shops and hotels. This confused my mother. While the people who accompanied us waited to hear our awe-stricken comments, I heard her say politely, " Surely Niagara can't be much finer than this." I gripped her hand hard and hoped that no one had noticed that the Governor-General's mother had not recognised Niagara when she saw it.

Only the other day I received from a friend in Ontario a book called *The Unknown Country*, a history of Canada and her people, by Bruce Hutchison. I wish I could have had that book with me when I was in Canada. It is a shaming thing to have to confess, but I knew practically nothing about the history of that great land, and my ignorance, I fear, is shared by many in Britain.

One night at a dinner-party, Mr. Mackenzie King repeated to me a passage from Francis Parkman :

" In these ancient wilds, to whose ever-verdant antiquity the pyramids are young and Nineveh a mushroom of yesterday ; when the wanderer of the Odyssey, could he have urged his pilgrimage so far, would have surveyed the same grand and stern monotony, the same dark sweep of melancholy woods—here, while New England was a solitude, and the settlers of Virginia scarcely dared venture inland beyond the sound of a cannon-shot, Champlain was planting on shores and islands the emblem of his faith."

The words went to my head like wine, and the moment I got home I demanded of John where I could get the book containing them. He at once went to a book-case and got me out two large volumes which I read with avidity. What was even more interesting than Francis Parkman was to listen to J. B. discoursing on Canada. He had always been interested in it as a country and now he was acquiring for it an affection that deepened with the years, and made the thought of leaving it when his term of office approached its end a real sorrow.

In the middle of June Walter arrived in Ottawa. He had only about three weeks to spend, but they were full and satisfying weeks.

It was sad to leave Ottawa where we had received so much kindness, but the friends we made there are still our friends and our lives are the richer because of it.

After Walter had had a few days in Ottawa we all set off for Murray Bay in the Province of Quebec, only the family, and Beatrice Spencer-Smith and Gordon Rivers-Smith.

The train stood in a siding that looked like an Alpine meadow.

Murray Bay lies at the mouth of the St. Lawrence, backed by the Laurentian, with beautiful rolling country all round it. The snake-fences intrigued me, and the silver spires of the many village churches. A lot of people have houses in Murray Bay and spend the summer there, and there are a few old houses. We were charmed to see the inside of a Quebec manor, and meet its Seigneur. A high white fence shut in a beautiful old garden with many great trees, shady walks, and old-fashioned flowers. The house was pleasantly shabby and full of the scent of lilac. There was a portrait by Raeburn over the dining-room mantelpiece of the man who built the house in 1790, Colonel John Nairn. Our hostess asked me if I would care to read his ' Letters,' and let me have the book away with me. I found it most interesting and there were some delicious bits in the letters. This, " Pray allow me to sink into poetry to help fill this paper," and his advice to his son, " All our family have ever been temperate, not practising even the Debauchery of smoking tobacco, a nasty Dutch custom, a forerunner of idleness and drunkenness; therefore, Jack, let us hear no more of your handling your pipe, but handle well your fuzee, your sword, your pen and your books," An odd thing about *Murray Bay* is that many of the people—*habitants* they are called—have Highland names. To be called Macgillivray and have no English seems strange. The reason for it is that a Highland regiment—many of whom had fought at Culloden—was disbanded there, and instead of returning to their native land married French wives and settled down where they were.

The *habitant* is a handy man. He buys almost nothing. He is a carpenter, farmer, blacksmith; his wife is weaver and tailor. The waggon he drives is his handiwork, so is the harness; the homespun cloth of his suit is made by his wife from the wool of his own sheep. The women make not only homespun cloth, but linen, straw hats, gloves, candles, soap. Where there are maple-trees the *habitant* provides his own sugar. Tobacco grows in his garden. His thrift is prodigious. We found them friendly people, the French Canadians, retaining some of the courtesy of the race from which they spring.

One evening a small village entertained our party to an open-air concert. The buggies they sent to meet us were wreathed in lilac, as was the rather coggly platform on which we sat. The performers were rather shy at first, but the *curé*, acting as *compère*, encouraged them and they sang very well. The only songs I recognised were 'Alouette' and 'Malbrouck.'

Before we left, John spoke to them in French, saying how much we were enjoying staying in their midst and thanking them for their kindness, and we parted in an atmosphere of great friendliness.

We were all looking forward to our stay at The Citadel, Quebec, the summer residence of Canada's Governor-General, and I had been reading everything I could find about the history of the town, and re-reading Willa Cather's beautiful *Shadows on the Rock*.

The Rock and the River, how many they have seen come and go since Cartier on August 10th, 1535, sailed up the river and named it St. Lawrence, because it was the feast day of that holy man. Next, a century later, came Champlain in his little lonely ship, seeing no life but the wild birds and the white whales turning over in the sunlight. Then Frontenac of the wild heart, and Montcalm, whose life was like " a white banner of honour before men."

In June 1759, James Wolfe, the youngest general in the British army, " a frail young man with sad brooding eyes," first saw the rock of Quebec from the river. He knew that to take the rock would be to take Canada, to make North America British. He took it and died. His monument bears the shortest and most eloquent of epitaphs : *Here died Wolfe victorious.*

The children today playing round the Monument as likely as not speak no English. Bruce Hutchison says, " The 60,000 Frenchmen conquered by Wolfe have grown to more than 3,000,000, about a third of the Canadian nation, and at the present rate of fertility will some day be the largest part. Wolfe's victory has turned out to be no conquest but a union, not yet complete."

Quebec rises steeply in winding little streets from the Lower Town to the Upper Town and, higher, to The Citadel. The barracks are alongside, and every day at a certain time a military band plays before the front door when the Governor-General is in residence.

There is nothing from the outside to make one think The Citadel is anything but a part of the barracks. Inside, the house has a charm that takes possession of one. It is neither large nor imposing, but extraordinarily lovable. The dining-room is on the ground floor, the walls painted with battle scenes. Upstairs is the drawing-room, with fine eighteenth-century furniture, and the ballroom, rather gloomy in the day-time.

Some years ago, I think in Lord Willingdon's time, a new room was added, a sun-trap of a room, built out on the edge of the cliff above the St. Lawrence, with windows all along one side, quite the most charming room imaginable, full of flowers and light. From it, by a door at the far end, you step out on to a long terrace, rather like the deck of a ship. It was a delight to walk up and down there in the early morning sunshine and gaze widely round at the superb view, and in the darkening to watch the lights twinkle out on the ships and across the river in Levis.

So fascinating was Quebec to explore and dream dreams in, and so many and various were the things to do, and the people we got to know so charming, that the date when we had to sail came all too quickly.

I seem to go on so monotonously asserting that the Canadian people are charming that I am reminded of a friend of mine who took a house in a certain small Scottish town, meaning to settle there if she liked it. After a few weeks she said she was going, and when I asked her why, replied :

" Well—I'm tired of being told that everyone I ask about is ' quite charming.' There is only a very limited amount of charm in the world and I have no reason to believe that this little town has the monopoly of it. Either the people here are stupidly unobservant or boringly charitable. Anyway, I've had enough of them."

In spite of this I maintain, what is the simple truth, that nicer people than the Canadians I never met. They are forthcoming without being gushing, generous almost to a fault, and the most loyal of friends.

CHAPTER XVI

JOURNEY'S END

WE had a lovely calm voyage home on our old friend, the *Duchess of Atholl*. It was packed with people, some of whom we knew. On board was a party of young people from various colleges making their first trip to Britain. We feared (not without reason) that Scotland would greet them shrouded in mist and rain, so it was a great gratification to all the Scots on board when we found ourselves sailing up the Clyde in the sunset of a perfect summer day, in scenes of almost theatrical beauty. We quite envied the youthful party when we saw them set off next morning from Greenock in charabancs for the Trossachs, with three weeks of sight-seeing before them. Probably many of them are back again in Britain, this time on sterner business.

We went straight up to London to give members of the family at home news of the absent ones, but in a week we were very contentedly settled down again in Peebles to enjoy what remained of the summer.

Before she left home Susie had made the family promise that if anything happened to any one of them she was to be told at once, nothing was to be kept from her. So, when the second boy was taken suddenly ill while staying with friends and was on the danger-list in a nursing-home for several days, a cable was sent to his parents.

They were touring in Victoria at the time and, when the cable arrived were leaving for an official garden-party. The couple spent a hideous afternoon, talking and smiling, their hearts cold with dread of what the next news would be. When, the tour finished, they returned to Ottawa,

Susie came home for a month or two, and took Billy back with her to recruit. Before leaving they came to Peebles, and we all went in to Edinburgh to see the first night of Barrie's play, *The Boy David*. The play had been so long expected and so often postponed that interest in it was keen, and the theatre was packed by an audience drawn from all parts of the kingdom. It is, perhaps, a better play to read than to see acted, and responsive as the audience was, most of us came away feeling that it had not quite come up to expectation.

J. B.'s letters—we always got two in a week—were a great interest, for he told us everything he was doing, and he saw to it that press-cuttings and photographs were sent to us continually.

Johnny, now quite recovered from East African germs, was in the service of the Hudson's Bay Company, and in 1937 came home to get some business training. He went to Dundee for six months to the School of Economics there. It was a complete change from anything he had previously known, but Dr. Bowie, the head of the College, by his kindness and interest made it a pleasant as well as a profitable time; and Johnny liked his fellow-students, and was befriended by many. He came to us every week-end, and that made a variety, and he specially enjoyed being back at Broughton, the happy hunting-ground of his childhood, where his patient feet had worn a path along the grassy bank of Biggar Water as he fished there every day. It was a treat to him to climb again with Walter the Broughton heights, and wander in the many green glens.

It was in that summer that J. B. had his trip to the Arctic. He was the first Governor-General to journey so far and attempt so much.

Dr. Jonathan Meakins said of him : " I have often heard

it said that he was frail. Yes, perhaps : frail as a rapier is, compared to a battle-axe."

There was a quality of Toledo steel about John. At sixty he was as swift on the hills as he had been at twenty ; he could leave men of half his age gasping. Perhaps because he was so far from being paunchy or puffy he always had a look of youth ; he kept his hair, and his eyes were as keen as a hawk's.

This journey was one of the wonderful experiences of his life, with its aeroplane flights to the frozen North and by canoe down virgin rivers. He had a passion for wild country and vast spaces, and it is fitting that thousands of square miles of wilderness is now a park bearing his name.

The marvellous thing was that he kept well all through this trek—and he did not grudge having to pay for it later.

The Coronation brought many of our Canadian friends to London and some of them journeyed up to Scotland and visited us, a kindness we greatly appreciated.

All that summer Mother was amazingly well and vigorous, untiring in entertaining, enjoying her friends to the full. She and I were all over the place opening garden-fêtes, and wherever she went she found old friends and made new ones.

In August she celebrated her eightieth birthday. Many things combined to make it a happy day. We had Johnny with us, and some of our best-liked relations motored many miles to do honour to the occasion ; presents poured in, and while we were at tea a cable came from John in the Arctic.

We went back to Peebles in the beginning of October, and as the winter began we realised, while refusing to admit it even to ourselves, that our mother was failing.

The asthma was troublesome and her strength to resist was weakening.

She changed in the last few months, becoming oddly like her mother, rather aloof and unapproachable. She withdrew herself; of all her multitude of friends she wanted none except the two who had been her constant companions for so many years, and with us she preferred to talk of the past and the people who had filled her life then.

She still went with me everywhere, but it was no longer a pleasure. One felt she was making herself do it so as not to fail me. About a fortnight before she died, returning very tired from some function, she said, " My dear, you and I'll have to split partnership."

She was only about a week in bed, not very ill—the doctor said he had often seen her worse—but she seemed to have lost the desire to live. Something was drawing her away from us—and she was content to go.

On her last day on earth she woke from a short sleep with a look on her face of utter content, the look we had seen long years before when she held the youngest of us in her arms. When I leant over her she said, " It was Alastair, he came and lay down beside me," and we wondered if she were being given back all she had lost.

CHAPTER XVII

> " Nay, but a dream I had
> Of a world all mad. . . ."
> WALTER DE LA MARE.

THE house seemed empty without Mother. To the end she had been at the head of things, a born home-maker, and now I had to struggle on alone. It was fortunate that I had then (and—miraculous as it may seem—still have) such efficient help.

We were in London for the New Year to see Johnny depart for Canada, to begin his work with the Hudson's Bay Company in Winnipeg. In April we met Alice and Brian in Stratford-on-Avon and were refreshed by a good draught of Shakespeare.

We were expecting both John and Susie home that summer. Susie came in June, John following a few weeks later. In July, Johnny, in Winnipeg, got sudden orders to go to Baffin Land for a year to learn something of the work of the Hudson's Bay Company in the Arctic. His father decided that Susie must see him before he left, and sent him home by the *Queen Mary* for five days.

Walter and I motored to Elsfield to see him for one night, and then he was off. Alastair (then at Christ Church) went with him to spend his summer vacation in Canada, and saw him off in the *Nascopie* from Montreal. For a whole year he could send no letters, nor receive any, but once in a while he could communicate with his parents by wireless.

Shortly after J. B. reached home he was installed as Lord Chancellor of Edinburgh University, and we were there as a family for the occasion. It was quite a memorable one, for there were present three Scottish Governors-General, and John, as Lord Chancellor, gave Lord Linlithgow, Viceroy of India, and Lord Gowrie, Governor-General of Australia, the degree of LL.D. He also had the pleasure of giving it to his great friend, Violet Markham.

A large luncheon-party followed the ceremony, with many speeches, then a garden-party, a dinner-party, and an evening reception. It was a wearing day for John, who had not only to make two quite long speeches, but had to talk continually for hours, and he did not look fit for it. One noticed old friends who had not seen him for some years looking anxiously at him.

The next day Susie and the children went home, but John wanted to have a day or two alone with us at Peebles. We motored back by way of the Glasgow Exhibition, which he had promised to visit. We somehow went in at the wrong gate and missed the officials who were there to welcome John, so we could wander through the Exhibition by ourselves, seeing the things we specially wanted to see. John was particularly glad to meet the Mounties in the Canadian Section, and we had the good luck to run into some of Knox's people, who and come that day in the hope of seeing their old friend. Finally we were discovered and taken off to lunch with some of the ' high heid yins '—and that was very pleasant too.

Then we set off for home.

Partly because it was one of his ' well ' days, and partly, I expect, because of the relief of getting a big job over, John that day seemed to throw from him every care. He had not travelled the road we took since he was a boy on a bicycle, and he pointed out to us each place of interest we passed, telling us its name and history. He sang songs and told us ridiculous stories. We knew him well in this mood. All his life, after long concentration, writing for hours, he would suddenly take what Mother called ' a daft turn ' and pour forth a stream of nonsense which reduced us all to helpless laughter. And hearing him, Walter and I realised how much we had missed those fits of nonsense.

In Canada he had so lived himself into the part he had to play, he had such a sense of the responsibility of his office, that he was wrapt away from us. It seems an absurd thing to say, but at Government House I never felt quite at ease in his company : there was a barrier—perhaps a shadow of that divinity that doth hedge a king—and one sometimes wondered rather sadly if we would ever get the John of other days back.

And here he was—not a day older than eighteen—calling us long-forgotten nicknames, reminding me of the time he had taken me, when I had first learned to ride a bicycle, to Broughton. We had divided the journey into three parts. The coal-mining places were Hades ; the Clyde Valley we called (most unjustly) Purgatory ; when we left the red roads of Lanarkshire and got on to the grey roads and among the green hills of Tweeddale we were in Paradise.

It was a wonderful journey that day from Glasgow, but as we neared home we fell silent, remembering the voice, now stilled, that would have welcomed us.

It had been arranged that when J. B. was home he would have a ' cure ' at Ruthin Castle in North Wales, but first he had much to attend to. He had brought home an invitation from the Prime Minister and Government of Canada to the King and Queen to visit Canada, and so convinced was he of the importance of such an event that he was determined to do all in his power to bring it to pass.

There was no question of the willingness of their Majesties to visit the Dominion, but Mr. Neville Chamberlain very naturally thought that in such uncertain times it was rash to arrange such a thing. But in the end by ' much asking ' J. B. prevailed, and it was decided that the visit should take place in the summer of 1939.

After Susie had seen John settled at Ruthin she departed to hold the fort in Canada, accompanied by Alice and Brian, and Hilda Grenfell. Walter and I kept John company when we could get away, and Billy was there part of the time. We stayed at a comfortable old inn at the Castle gates.

John liked the place, and found the doctors and nurses all that was kind and efficient. The treatment seemed to suit him, and it was a delight to see his face all smoothed out and almost plump, and he could eat with appetite and not suffer for it. He was always the tidiest of people. I asked his son William one day if he were feeling pretty poor at the moment. " Why ? " he said. " Am I looking so shabby ? It's because you're comparing me with my papa. Did you ever see anyone so smart ?—that grey suit and navy-blue and grey pull-over, and the discreet socks and tie, *and* the button-hole ! Did you know that the gardener sends him in one every morning and another in the evening ? "

We drove every afternoon to visit one of the numberless lovely places round, and often had tea in the Castle garden, and sometimes John read to us bits of the autobiography he was writing, which he called *Memory Hold-the-Door*.

The only thing that disturbed that halycon time was Munich. History will decide whether Neville Chamberlain did the wise thing, but in 1938 there were many angry and humiliated Britons. What seemed to me quite intolerable was the way people, who in their hysterical gratitude to their saviour were willing to kiss the hem of his garment, turned round and rent him when they found that our humilation had been for naught and we had to fight after all.

When things were very critical, Susie, in Canada, was naturally very anxious. One night, about midnight, John was roused to speak to her on the telephone. He did his best to reassure her, and finally said, forgetting the difference of five hours in the time, " Now go to bed, and don't worry." Upon which Susie replied, " I *can't* go to bed, it's only seven o'clock."

Things got very odd after that, and there was little for our comfort in the activities of Adolf Hitler. A feeling of foreboding was in all our hearts, and the departure of the King and Queen to Canada was perhaps the most cheering and steadying thing that happened in the summer of 1939. For eight months Canada had been preparing for the visit, every detail of the tour had been meticulously planned, every minute, almost, accounted for. Then, as will be remembered, they were delayed by icebergs and were late in arriving.

J. B. wrote : " We have been having an awful time in the last two days while our Monarch has been becalmed in a foggy ice-field. What induced the Atlantic suddenly to go Nazi ? It has meant a complete re-casting of plans, and I'm afraid it will give Their Majesties a terribly congested time in Ottawa . . . Spring has come with a bound. I have never seen England greener than our park. The tulips will be out in time, I think. Ottawa is at the moment a very beautiful city."

From the moment Their Majesties set foot in Quebec there was no doubt about the triumphant success of the tour. The Governor-General's train had been painted blue and silver and redecorated throughout, and in it our King and Queen went through the length and breadth of

Canada, winning the hearts of all who came in contact with them. It was quite common to find hundreds of people who had travelled many miles by car or buggy or on foot, standing in the night at different points simply to see the train pass, standing in silence in case their cheers might disturb the sleep of the weary travellers.

John could only tell us of the Ottawa part of the visit, and the good-byes at Halifax. For the time being his occupation was gone. He quoted Portia's speech :

> " ' So doth the greater glory dim the less.
> A substitute shines brightly as a king,
> Until a king be by ; and then his state
> Empties itself, as doth an inland brook
> Into the main of waters.'

" On Friday when Their Majesties arrived here it was rather a drizzling morning, but we decided on having the open state carriage at all costs. The eight-mile drive was a wonderful thing, for people had come in from all the little towns round about, and there must have been many thousand Americans. I, of course, could not go to the Senate Ceremony in the afternoon, but I believe it was a very impressive and dignified affair. Our state dinner in the evening went off very well, and since it was not big the King and Queen were able to talk to practically everybody.

" Next day, Saturday, we had the Trooping of the Colours in the morning in the central square. Then we went to the Judicature Building for the Queen to lay the foundation stone. I observed that one of the masons was a Scotsman and told the Queen, and she made a bee-line for him and took the King with her, and they went round talking to the mason. It was an unrehearsed effect which delighted the thousands of spectators. The Parliamentary dinner in the evening went off well. The great moment was when they appeared on the balcony of the Château Laurier.

There was an immense crowd below in the great square, all in the dark, for the floodlight was on the balcony. When the King and Queen appeared such a shout went up to heaven as I have never heard before. It was one of the great experiences of my life. . . . Yesterday morning, in beautiful weather, we had the unveiling of the War Memorial. The King spoke very well, as indeed he has done on every occasion since he landed. At the end the Queen told me that she wanted to go down among the troops, meaning the six thousand veterans, and in a minute we had disappeared in that vast mob—simply swallowed up. The police could not get near us, but I knew it was all right because the veterans kept admirable order. It was really extraordinarily touching, so many of them were Scots, some of them from Angus, and there were tears in their eyes as they looked at the Queen. One old fellow said to me, ' Eh, man, if Hitler could see this ! ' It was a wonderful proof of what a people's King means."

When it was all over J. B. wrote : " We joined the royal train about sixty miles from Halifax, and I had a long talk with the King. . . . The departure from Halifax was very impressive. It was a gorgeous evening, and the harbour is one of the most beautiful in the world. First went the Canadian destroyers, and then the *Empress*, with the tiny figures of Their Majesties on the bridge, and the grey, menacing cruisers following. . . . So that is that. It has been an amazing success. We took some big chances, but they all came off. I feel very much relieved and, as Mother used to say, ' we have great cause for thankfulness.'

" We have all fallen deeply in love with Their Majesties. . . ."

It had been arranged that Walter and I would go to Canada in July, and though everyone warned us that we were rash to attempt it, we were determined that nothing would daunton us—and off we went. I can never be sufficiently thankful that we did go, and were allowed to spend the last five weeks of peace as a family.

We sailed in the *Empress of Britain*, that lovely ship. Some of the passengers had been inspired to take the trip because of their interest in the Royal Tour.

We arrived in Quebec to great heat, and it was delightful to find ourselves in the cool and airy Citadel so fondly remembered.

All the household, except Colonel Eric Mackenzie and Mrs. Carruthers (Violet Markham), who to our delight was staying at the Citadel, had gone to Montreal for the day, to attend the wedding of Captain David Walker, the A.D.C., to Miss Willa Magee of that city.

When, late in the evening, the party returned, they were in high spirits, full of the happy wedding and the charm of the bride. The young couple were sailing the next day to spend the honeymoon in Fife, Captain Walker's home county.

We had a week in Quebec, a week of gorgeous weather and many excursions to places in the neighbourhood, and then we set off in the famous train (no longer blue and silver but back to its useful chocolate-brown) for a three-weeks' trip.

We were looking forward greatly to this trip. It was all new to Walter and me, and much of it was new to the others, for we were going right up to the North, to Churchill, to meet Johnny who was returning in the *Nascopie* from his year in the Arctic.

We were an entirely family party except for Robin Scott, the naval A.D.C., a delightful person, who looked after everybody and everything in the most efficient way.

When I woke that first morning, and lay looking out

on vast forests and great lakes while I dallied luxuriously with breakfast in bed I did feel a very fortunate person.

Winnipeg was our first place of call. All the others knew it well, but Walter and I were very pleased to be taken a drive round. One had somehow imagined Winnipeg as a sort of cow town; instead we found a city with wide streets full of great shops, many handsome buildings, a fine park, and a Zoo.

Later, we were attached to a train which ran about once a fortnight (I think) to Churchill, and we ambled along for two days and two nights. When we halted to get water and ice for the air-conditioning, all the passengers got out to walk about and talk to each other. There were all kinds —bontanists, biologists, school-teachers, trappers, hunters, Mounties—all taking the trip from Churchill in the *Nascopie*, as it carried stores for places like Hudson's Bay posts before the winter closed down on them.

We never tired looking out at the scenery, woods, clearings, and meadowland. Now and again we saw a village, a few houses, a small store, a tiny graveyard. For a time we passed through great flat fields of splendid crops which we hoped fervently would be safely gathered in. Before we reached Churchill we got into most curious country, stunted trees and miles of bent—what the Indians call ' the land of little sticks.'

Churchill itself seemed the end of creation, a place of wonderful clear light that gave the flowers growing over the sandy turf an extraordinary brilliance. The sea was dark green, and on the horizon lay what looked like a bank of cloud, but which, we were told, was ice.

A short distance by sea is Fort Prince of Wales, an eighteenth-century fort, taken by the French, and returned to us after Waterloo. We went out and looked at it; nobody lives on it now.

The evening after we arrived we ploughed through the sand on a sort of truck, the only means of conveyance, to meet the boat that was bringing Johnny. That was a night to remember !—the starlight, the breath-taking clear cold air, the faces of the Indians and the Eskimos, the growling of the huskie-dogs, the chunk-chunk of the blunt-nosed little *Nascopie*, coming nearer and nearer. We could make out Johnny standing ready to leap off, and in a few minutes we were all bundling back into the truck, eager to get into the warmth and light of the train and have a good look at our returned Ulysses.

To live for a year in a snowy waste, cut off entirely from letters, newspapers, books, and friends, hardly seems an ideal existence, but he insisted that he had been perfectly happy. And we could believe it, for from his childhood he had always liked to get away from what he called civilisation and live hard. While he was at Oxford he and two or three other undergraduates spent a month on deserted St. Kilda. Another vacation was spent working on a trawler. It was a very fortunate thing that his chief at the Baffin Land Port, a Newfoundlander, had proved the perfect companion, and the two had lived together in amity, and parted from each other with regret.

For the Eskimos Johnny had a great affection and respect; some of their work that he brought back, particularly the painting on ivory, was quite beautiful.

It was days before we finished asking and answering questions. When some one asked, " What did you think of Munich ? " and he said vaguely, " Munich ? What about it ? " we felt that there were points about living in Baffin Land.

Coming back from Churchill we stopped at various places where we got off tidily dressed, and John made speeches, and Susie (waited on by me, as her Lady-in-

Waiting had gone to England for a holiday) visited various Canadian Clubs and Women's Institute Meetings, and met the leading ladies of the district. At one place they had organised a picnic for us. We drove many miles in cars, and in a clearing in the forest near a lake were given a wonderful lunch. It was quite near the place where Grey Owl had lived.

One of the villages on the road had been christened Tweedsmuir. It was even smaller than its original on the banks of the Tweed.

At Edmonton we shopped at the Hudson's Bay Store, where you can buy anything from gorgeous furs to a sixpenny thriller, and were hospitably entertained at the house of the Lieutenant-Governor.

From Edmonton we went to Jasper to spend the week-end. Things that one has heard much about are apt not to come up to expectations, but the Rockies far surpassed anything I had imagined. Those great icy peaks, and the colour of the lakes, sometimes rose-pink, sometimes turquoise-blue, then green, quite took my breath away. We had a delightful afternoon driving to the Athabasca Glacier, and a whole day at Beaver Lake fishing—it must be confessed with little success. It was great excitement to see our first moose. It came out of the forest and posed for its picture like a film star. On our way home we met two big black bears walking on the highroad.

The hotel at Jaspar is a collection of log-huts of different sizes dotted about a great park of green velvet turf. There the guests sleep, and they feed in the central cabin, where there is a huge dining-room, as well as rooms for reading and writing, dancing and playing bridge. A holiday paradise !

It is difficult to get away from Peebles : we found that both the manager of the hotel and the station-master had been brought up there !

Leaving Jaspar with great reluctance, we set out for the Peace River. As it was the first time Their Excellencies had visited the district it had been arranged that we should spend a certain amount of time at all the larger places, but it was so distressing to pass without stopping at wayside stations, where a little group of people stood carrying flags and bunches of flowers, that Johnny and Alastair arranged with the engine-driver that he should warn us by a buzzer when we approached any station, and we would be ready to leap out.

At the larger stations all the people in the neighbourhood with cars were gathered—as well as some in buggies and on horseback—and we went round in a sort of procession to see the sights.

We saw on the banks of the Peace River the place where Sir Alexander Mackenzie spent the winter before setting out on his explorations. Some of the little townships were exactly like old Western films—one dusty street of wooden houses and a store with some horses in buggies tied up before it. The names, too, intrigued one, Dawson Creek, Pouce Coupé, Fort St. John. We visited a settlement of Sudeten Germans who had been got out of Hitler's clutches and were being given a chance to make a living in Canada. They were there with their wives and children, all classes—scientists, surgeons, clerks, labouring men, working with their hands, building their log-houses, getting their bits of ground in order. It was horribly pathetic to hear them sing our National Anthem.

How the scheme prospered I have never heard; it seemed to us at the time rather a desperate venture, but now, looking across the world from free and peaceful Canada to their own torn and tortured land, one would imagine that their sorrow would be largely mixed with gratitude.

The Peace River is a very wide district and many families live terribly isolated lives. Some are very poor. If their crops fail they have so little behind them that they can hardly help getting into debt, but they are not easily beaten.

Motoring long distances with people one had the chance to hear something of their lives. One prosperous-looking middle-aged couple told me how they had started their married life on a small farm in the back of beyond, many many miles from a neighbour. There was no doctor or nurse when the first baby was born. The wife must have been a plucky woman. When her husband was offered a job that would take him away from home weeks at a time, she said that was all right, so long as she had a gun. So she worked their bit of ground, did all the chores outside and in, shot what food was wanted for herself and the child, and kept everything going until her husband had enough to be able to live at home. No wonder they had prospered : they looked at each other in such a comradely way.

After we had visited a well-equipped little hospital a pretty young woman told us how it had been built. One Christmas her little boy had died because help was not forthcoming in time, and then and there she and her husband made up their minds that no other mother, if they could help it, would lose a child for want of medical skill. It was a scheme that appealed to everyone, and in a surprisingly short time they had raised enough money to build and endow a small cottage hospital.

Our last jaunt at Peace River was to Fort St. John. We crossed the mighty Peace on a raft which took us, cars and all. At that time Fort St. John was the last outpost of civilisation, now it is a part of the great Alaska Highway, and the quiet village with its few houses, an inn, and a store will be a humming hive of industry.

In Canada that summer, whoever we talked to, wherever we went, there was only one topic of conversation—the Royal Visit. No matter what we began to talk about we always ended there. Everyone had some story to tell about it.

One Englishwoman who had started 'Guides' in her district, told me that she made up her mind that her Guides would not miss what was probably their only chance of seeing the King and Queen. They were poor children, not very well equipped as Guides, for money was scarce in their homes, but that did not stop her. She got a railway truck from the officials, and the fathers of the girls put clean hay into it, and made bolsters for them to lean up against. Some people contributed money for any expenses and small treats they might have in the town, and others supplied food. The truck was linked up with a train and they started on their three-hundred-mile journey to the town which Their Majesties were going to visit. It was a very slow train, and they were much delayed, but they did arrive—just in time.

There were many companies of Guides drawn up, and my friend warned her little flock that though the Queen would probably not even glance in their direction they must stand as straight as if her eyes were on them. But, as it happened, the Queen came quite close to them, and perhaps she saw signs of the effort they had made to be present, anyway she smiled straight at them. My friend said, " We stood like ramrods, at least I hope we did, but our hearts were at her feet."

Very regretfully we left the Peace River and its friendly people, and in four days we were back in Ottawa.

All through the trip we had been well out of the way of newspapers, and though there was a wireless on the train we seldom listened in. J. B., of course, got cables from London which Robin decoded, but he did not speak of them, and when one is on the other side of the Atlantic one looks at Europe through the wrong end of a telescope.

When we were sitting down to luncheon at Government House the day we came back—a Tuesday it was—someone said, "Isn't there any news?" And Robin replied, "Rather bad news, I'm afraid; Germany and Russia have made a pact."

No one said anything more, and we went on eating.

But we were well aware of the seriousness of the news. Lord Maugham, then Lord Chancellor, who with his wife had arrived that day at Government House to spend a few days before going on to speak at various places, decided to return by the *Empress of Britain*, which was sailing from Quebec on the Saturday.

Walter and I had intended to motor from Ottawa to the States—I particularly wanted to see Vermont, because of Dorothy Canfield's books—but we reluctantly decided that we, too, would go back on the *Empress*.

The few days left to us in Ottawa were like an uneasy dream. The sun shone, everything was looking beautiful, kind friends were pouring invitations on us, but nothing seemed real.

The house was full of visitors, but we escaped when we could, and went out to the woods and picnicked together as a family.

On the Friday David Walker and his young wife arrived back from their honeymoon. That night at dinner we drank to their health and good fortune with spurious gaiety. (David Walker was to be taken prisoner at Dunkirk: Robin Scott to go down fighting gallantly and hopelessly on the *Greyhound*, off Crete.)

Later in the evening we had a little time alone with John and Susie, and said good-bye to them.

We left the next morning about 6 a.m. to catch the boat-train at Montreal, seen off by Robin and Johnny and Alastair. Feeling far from courageous I studied the faces of the other passengers on the boat-train, and decided that they were not the kind of people one would want to drown with. . . .

We reached London about 1 a.m. on the first night of the black-out and drove to the Langham, which had always been a sort of second home to us, and glad we were to find ourselves back in it.

The news in the papers next morning seemed slightly more reassuring, so I went out to buy some clothes. In Oxford Street the first edition of the evening papers announced that Germany had invaded Poland. It was a strange London that day. The shops were practically empty; the assistants standing in groups told each other the latest rumours. In reply to some remark of mine about the serious news, the tall young woman who was showing me clothes said bitterly, " My husband was killed in the last war, and my boy is just ready for this war."

We had hoped to go to Westwell to see Alice and Brian, but decided that we must leave for home the next morning.

One spot of brightness was Billy's presence at dinner that evening. He was in high spirits as he had just got engaged to Nesta Crozier, and, insisting that we must go out and see something, he dragged us to the Odeon to the film *The Spy in Black*.

There was only one other person in the balcony, a man, who presently rose and went out. Walter and Billy appeared to be enjoying themselves immensely, but to me it was all ghastly—the empty cinema, Conrad Veidt's sad face, the black-out waiting for us outside, the menace of war pressing one down.

I thought the film would never end, but at last we were out, and after scratching matches all over Leicester Square we fell up against a taxi which took us back to the hotel.

As we left Euston for Scotland that Saturday morning the station was packed with children, each with a label, setting off they knew not where. Next morning, while the Sabbath bells were ringing in the quiet town of Peebles, Mr. Chamberlain told us we were at war.

CHAPTER XVIII

" Men must endure
Their going hence, even as their coming hither;
Ripeness is all."

King Lear.

ON 4th September J. B. wrote : " . . . Well, the worst has happened—the Feuris Wolf, as Kipling used to say, is unleashed again—and yet, not the worst, for at any rate the air is clear, and we have a straightforward course before us."

And on the 11th : " On Saturday I got a letter from you written on the boat, in which you still cherish hopes of peace. Alas ! they came through the Ivory Gates. We are fairly in for it. Yesterday morning I was called out of bed to declare war on Germany. It has been rather a remarkable achievement of the Prime Minister, for by careful handling he has got Canada into the war without any dissension. The keenness is tremendous here, but it is a very quiet keenness, with no rhetoric about it, and all the more formidable for that.

" Life will be very much changed for all of us. John and Alastair will enlist in Canadian units. (They are acting as temporary A.D.C.'s at present.) Most of my time will be spent visiting troops. . . . It will be a curious existence with this big house half empty and undermanned. . . ."

2nd October. " Your letters and Walter's are an enormous comfort, for into the fantastic world in which we now live they bring a breath of familiar things. . . . Susie had a wonderful time in the Mid-west last week, and addressed enormous meetings. We had about eighty country school-teachers to tea on Saturday. We are trying to make Government House a centre of encouragement and advice. We have small week-end parties of people who ought to meet each other, and I think in that way we can do a lot of good. Susie has started a Government House working-party for the Red Cross. I am arranging to inspect a great deal of military work, especially in connection with the air, and am flying to a distance tomorrow to review some air units.

" John and Alastair go on steadily with their training . . . and now, my dear, I beseech you not to take on any unnecessary duties—you will have plenty of necessary ones. There is no need to advise you and Walter to keep up your spirits. No Buchan can ever be long depressed."

On the 4th of September we heard that the *Athenia* had been sunk, and from time to time other ships were attacked, and now and again a bomb fell in the Orkneys or Shetland, destroying a harmless cow, and once in Princes Street we heard the sound of guns and saw in the sky puffs of white smoke which, we learned later, had been an attack on our ships in the Forth. We veterans of the last war had dreaded a repetition of the long lists of casualites in each morning's paper, but except for the black-out and the evacuees, we found that everything that first winter was much as usual. In fact life became a far more interesting thing for many. Women got themselves into uniform as one thing or another, canteens were started, innumerable committees were formed; bridge-tournaments, whist-drives, and all sorts of entertainments were organised to raise funds, keeping everyone happy and cheerful.

In the end of October Walter and I took a few days off to attend William's wedding. He had been anxious to be married in the little Elsfield Church, and, as it was within easy reach of Nesta's home at Culham, so it was arranged.

The children's grandmother, Mrs. Norman Grosvenor,

at the urgent request of John and Susie, had removed herself and her household to Elsfield Manor for the duration of the war, and assisted by Alice, she was the hostess at the luncheon to which everyone was invited after the ceremony. It was supposed to be a quiet war-wedding with no invitations, but a surprisingly large crowd of relatives and friends managed to be present. The day was perfect, the young couple radiant, and our thoughts flew across the Atlantic, as we mentally jotted down every detail to tell the absent parents.

That first winter was remarkable for the severity, not of the war but of the weather. It was mild till Christmas, but with the New Year came a blizzard of snow, followed by a frost which froze everything that would freeze, and the cold lasted for months. But there was no scarcity of anything ; we had plenty of food and coal and petrol.

We were living at that time in a fool's paradise, listening to and half-believing the most fantastic tales. Hitler had almost no oil or petrol, that was why he did not attack us. Hitler was a rat in a trap, and the German people were on the point of revolting against their leaders. Some people actually believed that the German tanks were only tin, and that in fact all their equipment was 'ersatz' to a degree. Those were the days when we sang "Hang out the washing on the Siegfried Line," and advised Hitler to "Run, Adolf, run !" A 'phoney' war indeed !

J. B. in his letters never took this view. Writing on 13th November, he said : "It looks as if an attack on Holland were certain. At the Armistice Service on Saturday it was rather solemn to see the Belgian and Dutch Ministers place their wreaths on the Cenotaph, not knowing what was before their countries. . . . This has been a week-end of broadcasting. Susie and I broadcast on Armistice

Day, and yesterday I opened the campaign of the Red Cross with a broadcast. . . . I go on my footpath way, not ill but never well. I am ashamed to complain of those crumpled rose-leaves when so many people are lying on iron spikes."

In December we saw a photograph in *The Times* of General McNaughton and his staff, and recognised among them—Johnny.

J. B. wrote : " I am overjoyed to get a letter from you this morning. I know that old John will want to see you as soon as possible. You would get a great surprise when you saw his stately figure in *The Times*. It was certainly a dramatic landing. I must say we have cause to feel proud of Canada—her keenness and complete unity. She is a magnificent answer to the German sneers at the Empire, and the doubts of some of our own people. We have sent you a really great soldier in Andy McNaughton."

January 8th, 1940. " I am afraid I have been a most remiss correspondent, but since last Monday, when we left for the Maritimes, it has not been possible to write a letter. We found the climate down there milder than Ottawa, and very like Scotland. It was a most interesting time. I visited all the ships, both of the Royal and Canadian Navies, and went out to sea in a destroyer. I tramped in the snow round all the coast defences, and had a long day with the Air Force. We gave a dinner to the chief Service people, and I was very glad to see my friend, the Nova Scotian Prime Minister—Angus Macdonald. I had only one disappointment. I was going out with the Air Escort to accompany the convoy for the first part of its journey, but the morning dawned with a howling blizzard, and it was impossible for aeroplanes to go up.

" The most dramatic thing I did was to attend the Conference of the old merchant skippers before the convoy sailed. You never saw such magnificent fellows—engaged on one of the riskiest jobs on earth and perfectly placid about it ! I made them a short speech which seemed to go down well. When I looked at those men I felt that nothing on earth could defeat the British Empire."

In his last letter, written the night before his accident and received by me a week after his death, he told me of the things he had been doing for the last time, holding the New Year's Levee, and so on :

" There is always something melancholy in doing things for the last time, and my roots are deep in this country. It is like tearing up mandrakes !

" ... And now will you do me a great favour. I propose to publish my reminiscences next September, when I leave Canada. The book has got to be illustrated, and I want you to help me to get these illustrations. I know you have a good local photographer who could do the work.

I. Orpen's picture of Alastair photographed.

II. I want a good picture of the Upper Tweed Valley, which I can call ' The Gates of Tweedsmuir.' The one I would like best should be taken from the road somewhere between Wrae and Mossfennan ; where the Stanhope Hills come into view. Walter will know what I mean.

III. A photograph of my portrait done by Sholto Douglas in 1900. I am not quite sure about this, and I rather leave it to your discretion. It is the only thing I have for that time of my life.

" Before photographing, the portraits should be taken out of their frames. I hope this is not too much trouble for you. . . .

" Yesterday we had a very good sermon from Mr. Ferguson in St. Andrew's, and in the afternoon I had a long talk with the Cardinal.

" Alastair is slogging away at his work, hoping to go over with the second division. . . .

" Tomorrow we are giving our formal dinner for the new American Minister and his wife.

" I shall be greatly obliged if you will get me the pictures I want. These, and one of Elsfield, will complete my list. I have finished my novel (*Sick Heart River*) and my auto-biography, and am almost at the end of my children's book about Canada. This will leave me with a clear field for farewells in summer.

" Take great care of yourself, beloved Nan, and make Walter do the same.

" Much love

from John."

That was written on the Monday. On the Tuesday we got a cable from Susie saying that John had fallen and cut his head and was unconscious.

The Atlantic seemed very wide that week as we waited. But we could have done nothing for him had we been there. It was of Susie, of Alice and her brothers, that we thought with anguish.

John and Susie—the names were always coupled by their friends—sitting facing each other at their big writing-table in the library at Elsfield, working together in the garden, talking by the fire over the events of the day, and —our latest memory—standing gravely erect as the band played ' God Save the King.' It was impossible to think of them separated.

The cables at first were fairly cheerful, but on the Thursday night they talked of ' considerable anxiety,' and we knew that in spite of the almost miraculous skill of the doctors and the care that was being lavished on him, John was not going to recover.

In the strange, unreal days that followed his death Susie said she felt borne up by the sorrow and warm-hearted sympathy of the Canadian people. The Prime Minister and the Government made everything as easy for her as possible, and when she sailed for home Alastair was allowed to accompany her—a crowning mercy.

The tide of grief and sympathy extended even across the ocean, busy people took time they could ill spare to write me long letters, giving me details they knew I must crave for, and some of the women in St. Andrew's Presbyterian Church (which Mother and I had attended with John while in Ottawa) had the very kind thought of compiling for me an album of press-cuttings and photographs, a gift which will always be greatly valued.

Mr. Ferris Greenslet, writing of his old friend in his book *Under the Bridge*, says, " He made quite literally a million friends. When I went to Ottawa, the week of his death, porters, conductors, small shopkeepers, men in the street, spoke of him with broken voices."

That is what strikes one most in all that was said and written of him, the note of personal affection and loss.

To take two instances :

" It is the simple unadorned truth to say that we loved this man. There was that about him which made a universal appeal. We saw in him an emergence of that quality of life which in our own best moments we all long to possess."

A leader in *The Ottawa Journal* begins :

" This extraordinary grief for Lord Tweedsmuir, bowing alike the heads of the great and humble, coming from all races and classes and creeds, what does it tell ? Surely that life today, plagued though it be by demagogues and dictators, afflicted by strife and hate, and cursed by false philosophies and ideologies, still gives its heart in affection and homage to the best in man."

And the writer quotes Hilaire Belloc :

> " He does not die who can bequeath
> Some influence to the land he knows,
> Who dares, persistent, interwreathe
> Love permanent with the wild hedgerows.
> He does not die, but still remains,
> Substantiate with his darling plains."

Many beautiful things were said to us in the thousands of letters that came from all over the world, and they helped, for lovely words have a healing quality, but nothing touched me more than the simple sentence of a girl in a Princes Street shop.   I had been sending some cake and sweets to my nephews and she asked me to put my name and address on the back of the order.   I scribbled " Buchan, Peebles," and she said :

" Are you John Buchan's sister ? "

The tears that sprang to my eyes at the unexpected question answered her, and for a moment in that crowded shop we looked at each other sorrowfully, as she said :

" He must be an awful miss."

CHAPTER XIX

"Is it so small a thing
To have enjoyed the sun?"
MATTHEW ARNOLD.

IN that wintry spring, after John died, I found a haven
in my eyrie of a study looking down on Tweed. To
get away from everyone is a necessity for some people
when grief comes to them, and I was fortunate in having
an excuse to shut myself away for a little—a book to finish.

It had been begun in Canada, and continued inter-
mittently at home, but when my mother died it was laid
aside and forgotten. Now I was glad of it.

We were still, in the spring of 1940, telling ourselves
fairy-tales about the war, when, suddenly, Hitler struck,
and after that things seemed to go on happening almost
without a pause.

After Dunkirk, while the whole world held its breath
as the blast of the terrible ones was directed against our
Island, it is amazing to remember how calm we all were.

A woman once said to me about her daring little son,
" Poor Sandy hasna the sense to be fear't," and that in a
way was true of us. We had never seen our country torn
by war, as had France, as had Belgium, as had Poland.
But there was more in it than just the calm of ignorance.
It was faith in the God of our fathers and in our destiny
as a nation that held us up and made us certain that though
we might suffer and die our Empire *could* not be beaten.

As time went on all of us realised something of what
total war meant, and the richer and more comfortable we
had been the more we felt it. On the woman who had
always known an idle, fur-lined existence, with no need to
take thought for the morrow, with cars to take them

swiftly and smoothly wherever they wanted to go, accustomed to willing service, and the best of food and drink, the new conditions weighed heavily. Gradually comfort left them. Travelling lost its savour when it became an affair of standing for an hour waiting for an over-crowded bus, or sitting in a packed railway carriage. Food-rationing made much entertaining impossible, and clothes coupons did away with that resource of the rich—buying from boredom. How many hats have been bought and dresses ordered because it was a wet day and nothing much was happening?

As to the servant question! Domestic workers, for the great part, folded their tents like the Arabs and faded from our wistful gaze.

It was interesting to see how women stood up to this test. Many—the old, and others who were not strong—were forced to find refuge in hotels and boarding-houses. Others tackled the problem with spirit, closed all rooms not in use and, preferring a well-scrubbed table and earthenware to dim mahogany and smeared silver, took meals in the kitchen, where at least the food was hot, straight from the pot. Some are struggling on as best they can, feeling it always a burden, and hoping against hope that a limit will be set to their labours and a cook turn up from somewhere; and a few have no desire to go back to thraldom; they feel that at last their home is their own, and that, as someone wrote recently, they have discovered the freedom of the true family life.

The trouble that most of us find about war-time housekeeping is that it takes up such a vast deal of time. It means going to the shops directly after breakfast, and standing in queues waiting for our turn. We are all getting pulled to one side by lugging heavy baskets, but that matters nothing if we are lucky enough to take home some small extra that will make a meagre meal slightly more interesting. One is so apt to get into a routine with meals, and in our house you know what day of the week it is by what you get for breakfast.

It has taken a global war to teach some of us to cook, and when I found that by mixing beer with flour and treacle an excellent 'soggy' gingerbread was the result, I was as proud as if I had discovered penicillin.

There is one thing noticeable about war-shopping and that is the patience and cheerfulness of the shoppers. There is little or no grumbling, and when it is a case of no meat, no fish, and no points for spam, we take it as a joke.

Indeed we have little reason to grumble. We are not rushing out after a hard day's work, like the munition-workers, to pick up what is left ; and if we stand in a queue we stand in safety—unlike many women lately in the South of England. When we are so busy with chores inside and out, and our usual work to do as well, we have not so much time to worry vainly about our men in the fighting line. They are doing their job and we are doing ours, and we leave it at that. And if at times something —it may be a tale from a Polish woman of what happened in Warsaw, or a sentence in a paper, *The children in Greece are too weak to play*, or a press-correspondent's account of the endurance of our men in the jungle—brings home to us the background of horror against which we move, this dreadful disease of war that is ravaging the whole earth, well, the only thing to do is to try to work harder, to give more.

And if the worst happens, if the telegram comes that shatters all hope in the future and takes the sun from the sky, still a meal must be cooked, and dishes and pots washed, and we must not fail, because we are needed.

Many have learned that work is a bulwark against despair. It is true that there is no equality of sacrifice. Some have only known the discomforts of shortage of petrol, and social contacts curtailed, others have had their houses destroyed, and lost all that they held most dear.

We in our quiet country-town feel almost guiltily aware of our good fortune! The war in the air has hardly touched us. One night, returning from raiding Glasgow, the enemy jettisoned their incendiary bombs on the hills, ringing Peebles with fire, but no harm was done; and when they dropped land-mines they fell in glens where there was no human habitation.

On the morning after our experience with the incendiaries, walking along the High Street I heard two women discussing it. One was a rather woe-begone little matron, the other was a stalwart spinster. The matron was bewailing the war.

" It's an awfu' world that we're living in the noo. I would have been fair ill wi' fricht last night if Tam hadna got up and made me a cup o' tea," to which the stalwart spinster replied :

" Ay, but we hevna a' got a Tam."

It was said in such an unenvious tone—indeed I am not sure that there was not a self-congratulatory twinkle in her eyes—that I went on my way feeling that it was this spirit, this cheerful acceptance of facts, that was helping us to win the war.

In 1914 we seemed much nearer the war than we do now. There were many more troops to be seen, all the parks were covered with tents ; each battalion had its own band, so that the air was full of stirring music. The men were trained on the hills round the town, and drafts were constantly leaving for one or other of the battle-fronts. Often, in the middle of the night, we were wakened by the sound of marching feet, and the wail of the pipes playing ' Will ye no' come back again ? '

In this war Peebles has never been a centre for the training of troops. The Hydropathic was at once requisitioned as a hospital. All the halls in the town were taken over, but only occasionally have they been filled with troops. Instead of tents there are Nissen-huts in the parks, and they stand unoccupied for months at a time.

Being considered a safe place Peebles is packed with evacuees, some of whom have added interest to the life of the old burgh. In 1940 we welcomed Polish soldiers. I am not one who agrees with the verdict that Scots manners are bad, but sometimes, I admit, they are simply not there at all, and it did us all good to meet the grave courtesy of the Poles. The graceful swing of their cloaks, the sound of their voices, gave quite a foreign atmosphere to our town. Many of them knew nothing of what had happened to their families, and must have carried lonely, heavy hearts, but others were fortunate enough to be joined by their wives and children, who have quite settled down with us. There is now a Polish Cadet College in Black Barony, and in order to make a centre where all the Poles could meet, and talk, and play and eat together some ladies in the district got hold of a small hall, which they furnished, and which is run as a Polish Club, and much appreciated. Many soldiers come to spend a leave in Peebles : Canadians, Australians, New Zealanders, Americans.

We, naturally, see most of the Canadians, and very popular guests they are, at home in any company.

One wonders what is the attraction of our quiet town, but the men seem to enjoy simple pleasures, walking on the hills, golfing, or setting out hopefully with rod and line to try to lure trout from the Tweed.

It is good that there are such peaceful places, but some of us could almost find it in our hearts to envy the people who have been asked to bear the heat and burden of the day.

On April 16th, 1942, Walter and I arrived at King's Cross in the early morning and found London lifting its head after a night of dread. Many buildings were still burning, the streets were full of enormous holes, splintered glass lay everywhere, but the girls were going to their day's work in shops or offices, as neat and tidy as they could be, picking their way through the destruction to all appearance as placidly as if they were in a meadow of buttercups and daisies. In spirit we abased ourselves before them.

It was the same when at last we reached our hotel in Piccadilly; people were coming down calmly to breakfast, no one even mentioning that the night had been a disturbed one. When we went out to do some shopping we found at least one of the places we had meant to visit was gone, the whole corner a heap of rubble, but, to our astonishment, it seemed to be taken quite as a matter of course—nothing to make a fuss about. One talks of London as bearing the brunt, but many other places have borne much.

In Coventry, I remember seeing in the ruined Cathedral an attempt at an altar, adorned with primroses. Undefeated they looked, the meek blossoms.

We have never had greater reason for thinking nobly of the soul.

As a family the war—so far—has dealt mercifully with us. Like everyone else we are almost constantly anxious, and will be till the fighting stops and our men return, but looking back one remembers many good things; our family circle has been enlarged and our lives enriched, by the addition of Perdita, the small daughter of William and Nesta, and of Hope Gilmour of Ottawa, who became Alastair's wife in 1942.

For the last two years I have occupied my few leisure hours by writing down well-remembered things about my own and my brothers' childhood and youth. One evening, when Susie was staying with us, I read some of it aloud to her, and she urged me to go on with it, and I did, though it seems more than a little presumptuous to assume that people will be interested in such a far from sensational life as mine.

Few of us, perhaps, get the life that in youth we hoped for, and confidently expected, but most of us, I daresay, get the lives best suited to us, and I have little to complain of in mine. Even now, with things as they are, happy is not too rich a word to describe it.

Mrs. Oliphant in her 'Life' says something which I read as a schoolgirl and have never forgotten. She had a hard life if ever woman had, supporting by her writing the whole family (she tells how she made a hole in her third finger by constant holding of the pen), and watching them all die before she herself got away, yet she says (I quote from memory): "With no reason for it, with every reason against it, my heart still jumps up in the old unreasonable way, and I am happy."

" Werena ma hert licht I wad dee !"

To the happy man, it has been said, all times are times of thanksgiving, and it is with deep gratitude that this pilgrim looks back on the way that she has come.

INDEX